# ONCE UPON AN ISLAND

## A *COLLECTION OF SHORT FICTION, POETRY & NON-FICTION FROM NEW KEY WEST WRITERS*

Library of Congress Catalog Card Number: 97-68162

ISBN 1-57502-515-9

Printed in the USA by

**MORRIS PUBLISHING**

3212 East Highway 30 • Kearney, NE 68847 • 1-800-650-7888

# CONTENTS

ALLEN MEECE
*Captain Hell*     7

WILLIAM WILLIAMSON
*Scorpions*     15

ROSALIND BRACKENBURY
*The Hundred Dollar Kitty Cat*     21

THERESA FOLEY
*Blue Menace*     29

JUDY ADAMS
*Come With Us Now*     33

ROBIN ORLANDI
*The Place We Live*     41

J.T. EGGERS
*Island of Bones*     45

BARBARA BOWERS
*The Cuban Godfather*     51

DEANNA O'SHAUGHNESSY
*To The Keys*     57

KIRBY CONGDON
*Two Gentleman in Bonds*     63

MARGIT BISZTRAY
*I, Olivia*     69

DANNE HUGHES
*For Zeb, Age Two*     77

DEANNA O'SHAUGHNESSY
*The Princess and The Pirates*     81

WILLIAM WILLIAMSON
*A Better Time, A Better Place*     89

ROBIN ORLANDI
*Hello Spring Break*                                                95

KIRBY CONGDON
*Rural Delivery*                                                    99

JUDY ADAMS
*And She Dialed 0*                                                  105

DANNE HUGHES
*Small Craft Warnings*                                             113

ALLEN MEECE
*Armando, Sculptor*                                                117

BARBARA BOWERS
*Fort Jefferson in the Dry Tortugas: Paradise or Prison?*   125

ROSALIND BRACKENBURY
*Lies*                                                            133

THERESA FOLEY
*Last Night in Paradise*                                          139

AUTHOR BIOGRAPHIES                                                149

4

# CAPTAIN HELL

## ALLEN MEECE

I used to drink but things happened to me. Take this, for instance. "I think Adam knows how to navigate," said the Hot Dog Man to a bland middle class manager-type who was out of place at the Schooner Wharf bar. He was forty-five and wore Sebago deck moccasins like none of us bothered to buy. With his white Bermudas he belonged in the Pier House with the other boat-owners.

"That's right," I said. I'd had a few beers. I was a shrimper on the "Henny Penny" and wanted to get off the rock for a while. My captain wasn't catching shit and was holed-up on land, drinking and screwing.

I'd studied the charts we'd sailed across but never used "navigation" on them. Shrimpers go where we want to go, same's you go across town without drawing lines on a map. I could get where I wanted to go and if owners call that navigation, then I was a navigator.

"This is John Hell and he needs somebody to navigate his boat down to Gitmo."

"Glad to meet you, Hell. I've been to Gitmo before." I'd spent a couple of days there on my destroyer when I was in the Navy.

He was impressed. He came closer and said what he wanted to do.

"I have to leave at midnight. My vacation time is almost over and I have to be back on the job in five days. I'm in charge of the civil servants down in Gitmo."

"There's a lotta water between here and Guantanamo," I said.

It was a seven hundred mile trip. The summer trades were good out of the northeast so we wouldn't have to tack much. It would take six days if we averaged five knots round the clock and nothing broke.

"I'm going to motor-sail when the wind's light."

Motor sailing. Might add two knots to our speed. I wish I'd known he would only run the diesel while I was trying to sleep.

"Yeah, that'll help," I said, knowing it wouldn't make much difference but not wanting to argue with the dude. Let him think he could do it in five days. Once you get out there, delusions don't work. We drank beer together to get to know each other. Like you can get to know somebody when you've been drinking.

"Okay," I said. "I'll get my stuff and see you on the boat."

Four days later, after being lost and fatigued and breaking equipment and arguing every detail, we were sailing down the Windward Passage a day behind schedule, just as I predicted. The swells were rolling high under a windy blue sky that blew straight out of our desired course.

"Tack east until you see Haiti and then tack west. We want to stay away from Cuba." I emphasized the obvious course because Hell had been stubbornly hugging the Cuban shoreline. I went below to sleep.

This was in 1986, when Cuba was linked with Russia and very hostile to American vessels in their waters.

When I came up for watch I peeped over the coaming and saw the hills of Cuba three miles away. I saw trucks driving the roads of Baracoa and a mill on the shore making smoke.

The novice captain was terrified of losing sight of land and/or deliberately trying to get us arrested. He probably wants to cause an international incident as an excuse for being late returning from leave. He wants fame and a cocktail story too. My welfare is the last thing on his pea brain.

"We're about three miles offshore, Hell. Better tack."

"No, it looks more like five miles."

"Goddam it, when you can see people on the goddam beach, you're within three miles. Now tack this sonofabitch!"

I threw off the mainsheet and stood there, hoping his eyes would twitch so I could hit him real hard.

"It's your turn at the wheel," he said coolly.

I was ready for a surprise move as he slid past me but he accepted physical domination instead of reason. I steered offshore.

He watched me. Perversely, he wanted me to boss him around some more but I wouldn't. You couldn't pay me enough to boss his ass around.

He saw something behind me.

"There's a boat coming after us."

I looked around. He was right.

"Trim the sails! I'm going to bear off and gain speed. See if you can start the engine."

The chasing boat was pumping the swells while we were slicing through them like a French knife. The pursuer wasn't too good, just a fishing boat with bluff bows. I thought we could outrun it.

"The diesel's dead, we're sailing for our lives," said Hell, melodramatically. He was creating cocktail stories on the spot.

We gave the Cubans a race. The Morgan had good sails that filled with power and drove her through the swells like a giant ballerina.

But they closed the range until we heard three cracks from a rifle, "Pat, Pat, Tap!"

"Hell, get down under the gun'l!"

I wanted to stretch it out and make sure they could catch us. The rifleman couldn't target us from his bouncing boat until he got a lot closer.

"No, they're shooting at us." He cast-off the main halyard and the mainsail went limp.

They had us. Hell was getting the tardy slip he wanted and I was going to rot in a foreign dungeon, without benefit of due process if the propaganda was right.

The patrol boat towed us through a long crooked channel through two miles of shallow water to a dock at the town of Moa. A Russian freighter named "Hero Admiral Gorky" was moored there. We were in the hands of a very communist country.

"Calling United States Coast Guard, this is the sloop Hellfire en route to Guantanamo Bay Naval Base. We were intercepted and are being towed into Cuba by Cuban Navy. Request assistance, request assistance."

Captain Hell kept repeating his message until the Hellfire was tied to the dock and a man came aboard and took his microphone away.

A rifle squad of Frontier Guards came aboard and wanted to do a routine drug search.

Hell said, "Okay, but would you please take off your dirty boots first?"

I gritted my teeth at his impudence and went up into the bows to distance myself from him in the eyes of the Cubans.

The soldiers found nothing, A doctor and a port official came aboard to check our health and documents. My tension was relieved when they produced a student composition book as a port registry. No foreign yachts had been to Moa before. They told us not to leave the boat and stationed a twenty-four-hour armed guard on the dock.

That concluded the formalities of entering the communist port. It was getting dark. I offered the port official, who seemed like a nice guy, an American cigarette which he accepted with relish. I lit it with the last of my matches and asked him if I could buy more matches nearby. He refused permission to leave the boat.

The harbor at Moa was an eerie place after dark. A steel mill clanked and banged and smoked all night and melted pieces from the surrounding junkyard into steel. Ragged, dirty young men wandered the dark scrap heaps stealing junk. Our guard wasn't to confine us but to protect us.

A car's headlights shone onto the dock. Our guard cocked his Kalashnikov and went forward to challenge the vehicle. It was the port official coming to check on us. He came alongside and had something for me, a tiny matchbox. Inside were six matches, half an inch long, made of straw with dots of sulphur on the ends. I realized the extent of the poverty that America forced on this country. We had a cigarette together and tried to make small talk but his English was bad and I had no Spanish. We called it a night.

In the morning the decks were covered in soot. Hell ran up the American flag to the spreaders and rigged a chrome water pump to spray seawater on the deck as he danced a sailor's hornpipe, deliriously showing American gadgetry to poor Cubans. That's when I understood the shame of middle-class materialism. Their biggest joy in life is showing shiny junk to poor people like a brat on the block who loves a new bike for the longing that it brings to the good kids' eyes, kids with a goodness he'll never possess. I wanted off that boat. I was serving Hell and I hated it.

The port sent a mechanic to fix our diesel. He found the 0-ring seal in the fuel filter was crimped and letting air in the fuel line. He worked four hours and Hell gave him an old brass water faucet worth two dollars. I thought I'd seen it all but Hell never stopped disgusting me.

The port asked the fair price of three hundred dollars in hard American currency for towing, docking and fixing us. Hell was broke and asked if I had any money. I gritted my teeth, which were ground down to stumps by now, and loaned him a hundred and fifty bucks to get me out of the jam he got us into.

Surprisingly, they accepted the half-payment. They even seemed anxious to get rid of Hellfire. Smart people. A patrol boat guided us out the channel and to the Windward Passage.

This time Hell didn't tack the coastline but sailed toward Haiti like I had told him the first time.

That night, at the bottom of the Windward Passage, the trades roared and high swells swept in from the open Caribbean. I was sleeping comfortably with the boat's rollicking gallop while the big sloop ran at hull speed. The only thing better than sex to a sailor is hull speed. The voyage was racing to an end.

As Hellfire rounded the bottom corner of Cuba, a boat's lights appeared on an intercept course. I was forced awake by the diesel's turning on and racing at maximum rpm. Hell was off to the races again.

Up on deck, Pandora's box was open and pandemonium was loose. Hell was being drenched by every swell that sluiced by and his face was a blank mask of hypnotized fear.

"The Cubans are after us!" he screamed. "Pull in the ropes before they foul the propeller!"

Under the push of the full-speed diesel and the straining sails, the prow was diving into swells and dislodging the docklines that were secured in the bow. They trailed overboard and a long ways astern.

I gauged the chance of a man working up there of going overboard to be about ninety percent. I gauged the ability of Hell to recover a man overboard as nil. I rigged myself a tight safety line and looked at the other boat's lights. They were dim, like a little fishing boat's, and they hadn't turned to follow fleeing Hell.

"Get your ass up there before they foul the prop! Quick! NOW! We can't let'em get us again!"

I carefully went forward and tried to haul the rope but our speed was putting heavy drag on it. He'd have to slow down, period.

"Slow down!" I yelled over the diesel and wind and surf.

He was fixed in fear. I went closer to make sure he heard. I had to force Hell to listen.

"Slow down! If the rope catches the prop it'll break it off or rip out the stuffing box and sink us. Slow down! Look at the other boat! It's breaking off the chase." I played along with the madman to save the boat and me.

Hell had trouble telling a boat's course by looking at its lights but after a minute he came back to his normal version of pseudo-reality and idled the diesel. I hauled in a hundred feet of line and passed it into the forepeak where it couldn't bother us again. It was badly chewed but for some reason the prop never got a full bite or we could've been goners.

"Thank you Gee-sus," I said, copying the old-time preachers. I meant it.

# Captain Hell

It was my turn at the wheel and I confess, I was knackered. Hell's insom-nomaniacal two-hour watches with their twelve shift-changes a day were taking their toll on me. My eyes were open but the images weren't coming through right. The white compass card under the red binnacle light glowed like a New England village covered in snow at Christmas-time. I looked at the church steeples and the numbers lying in the snowy streets, numbers like 180, 0 and 270. I'm going to fly down to that village and go into that nice house on the corner with a picket fence and sleep. But 180 sounds familiar. It means south, I think.

I shake my head and look away. I seem to be on a sailboat in a sloppy blind night. Which illusion's real? Reality is a tiny spark in my soul but where is this body located? Is this body me?

The compass still shows the Christmas card town. Is that here or is here there? What does "here" mean? I have no way of knowing.

I muster my senses one by one. I touch fiberglass and smell the wind and turn the spreader lights on to examine the sails. I steer upwind to see if they luff when pinched and are not just white images painted on my retinas.

BANG, Whap! The main jibes over, booming hard, "Here's your reality, mister!"

I'm back from my trip to the non-material dimensions.

If I can make it through this last watch, the trip'll be over. Let everything sleep but your eyes. Look at the black ahead, look at the compass. Ignore the churches. Don't stare, you'll lose focus. Keep your eyes moving. Be mechanical, be an autopilot, don't try to keep your whole body awake, you can't. Conserve the energy you've got left. An hour and a half to go. Ninety tiny minutes. They get longer, slower. Each one becomes fifteen. They go slower. This watch is the rest of your life.

"I'm bein' followed by a moodshadow. Moodshadow, moodshadow an me." You sing to hear a voice, to break the entrancing tedium but the words come out reflecting Hell's problem. You think of other places to escape the hypnotism here.

Tomorrow I'll be on Gitmo, his turf. Will that make things better between us? He supports a second wife and her son. You respect the first wife for leaving, can imagine no more miserable existence than living with Hell. But he's probably better on land, where they're used to crazy stuff. Land offers a huge margin for error. This trip's been a strain on his presumed omniscience.

12

In the first light of morning I pull out Hell's treasured Bendix radio direction finder that his dad perversely bequeathed to him. Hell's heirloom is a dangerous instrument that gives bad plots and it would've put us on the rocks many times if I'd believed its faulty readings. Now it receives a strong signal. Gitmo is due north and very close.

I turn the boat and head in. The green bluffs of Cuba come out of the hazy dawn. A black rubber patrol boat comes out to escort us into port and we feel honored. We imagine they respect us intrepid voyagers as Vikings.

When we are moored firmly to land and the voyage is actually over, from somewhere comes the imaginary voice of Hell's director.

"OK, everybody ready? All the props in place? Get those tin cans out of the cockpit, we want the boat to look shiny new. OK actors; ACTION!"

His wife and stepson come down to the dock. She hugs him. He gives her his idea of a masculine kiss and she's properly excited about the beauty of his racing sloop.

"Is it big enough?" He asks in manly fashion.

"Ooh, it's huge." She knows him.

His stepson likes the boat but knows it's not going to be any fun, just a place to get ordered around and told you're not doing it right, as Hell plays the expert captain. I get the feeling he doesn't like anything his stepdad likes. Smart kid.

We go to his office, which he claims is "bigger than the base commander's." He's on familiar bragging ground. His staff gathers around to hear of the trip and he tells them about enemy captivity without one word about how I made the trip work. I was basically a passenger, as he told it.

I wanted to get one of his underlings aside and clue them in but Hell didn't let me talk to anybody alone.

We went to his house. "Isn't it big? Big as the base commander's. Not as nice but almost as big. We're going to get some Jamaicans to landscape it. It'll be as nice as a Navy captain's."

I was looking at a child's shiny bicycle.

"I can't tell you how happy I am for you, captain. You really live a good life." I tried to convey subtle contempt. I'd had enough. He was worse on land.

"I'd love to stay longer and fix up the boat interior but I'm missing my girlfriend and Key West." I had planned on staying in Gitmo a week and getting to know it but not now. All you need to know about a place is whether or not Hell lives in it.

He offered me the use of his spare bedroom but I insisted on sleeping on the boat even though I wanted off it before. It was better than sleeping in Hell's house.

In the quiet harbor after nightfall a couple of base policemen came by. I started to clue them in on Hell but they were bored by that topic. They knew all about him, he was the base joke and they weren't the kind of men that talked about sick stuff. I thought I had a patent on bullshit detectors but the people of this narrow, armed camp were way ahead of me.

They offered to bring me a six-pack of beer to wash the salt from my throat but I refused. I actually refused.

When they drove away it was just me and Hellfire.

"I pity you old girl. You're a good boat and now you'll never be sailed right. You were good out on the Great Banks and you'll always have that. More than a lot of Morgans have, tied up to the back of mansions like floating ornaments."

Quiet ripples along her graceful waterline. She's resting.

The first night in port, especially after a hard trip, would normally be an occasion for my getting uproariously drunk. But that's what started this trip and other trips just as bad. I was ready to straighten my course.

I lowered an object to the bottom on a rope with a note attached and tied it off under the counter where he wouldn't find it for a while. I wrote, "Here's a lovely sea anchor for you Captain Hell, it's a genuine Bendix," and flew to Key West in the morning.

# SCORPIONS

*WILLIAM WILLIAMSON*

I remember how intimidated I felt when dad pushed me through the sagging wooden gate to meet his Aunt Lela the first time. A weathered picket fence surrounded her cottage. Lela seemed as ancient and worn out as her surroundings.

She was resting in a rocking chair, facing the narrow brick street, the curved armrests polished so smooth the wooden grain was a blurred enamel. Both hands were hidden in a large bowl on her lap. She didn't smile, get up, or even slow the rhythm of her rocking, watching us approach. When I reached the first crumbling step, she reached down beside her and grabbed a handful of string beans from a paper sack on the porch.

The way she looked at us, or looked right through us, I thought dad was mistaken and we were at the wrong house. Dad hadn't seen Lela in over ten years, but her name was mentioned more times in the last month than I heard in my life. For weeks dad and his girlfriend argued over his decision to work the shrimp boats during the summer. Rena, my dad's girlfriend, didn't want to be responsible for me all summer. That was settled when he remembered Lela.

Dad said he could make a lot of money under the table while still collecting his unemployment checks. Rena was doubtful, warning him, "Yeah, you could make a lot of money if you could stay sober. Which you can't."

They made a deal. If dad could go sober for a week, she would support his decision to work the boats in Key West. Dad never quit drinking, but the week passed without Rena suspecting anything. He ate a lot of onions and garlic that week.

Lela stared at me, dark, beaded pupils in a cloudy sea, void of any emotion. Her leathery, worn face housed deep wrinkles and dark sunspots, great splotches of brown hanging on her loose skin like leprosy. Her grey hair with white streaks was pulled back in a short ponytail with a pink rubberband. She wore a thin, faded sleeveless dress clinging to her thighs, draping her heavy, varicosed legs. The raised veins trailed like a meandering river. Her knee-high hose were bunched around her swollen ankles above cotton slippers.

Initially, I was shocked by the dark sunspots masking her face and flabby arms till I noticed what a very big woman she was. She seemed to swallow her rocking chair. Her girth spilled out the sides so tight I questioned whether she could get up and go inside her house. Maybe she lived in her chair every minute of the day.

I tried to peer through the dusty screen door, but it was like looking into a black shadow. The place smelled old. She smelled like the old house and the old house smelled like her. After a week I think I smelled like it too.

Hooked on the armrest of her chair was a rosewood cane, the curved handle was taped and soiled, the rubber stopper worn completely to the wood on the bottom. I guessed she could get up if she had a cane to walk with.

I stopped at the steps, not wanting to be the first on the porch. A gecko lizard froze, studying me to see if I was a concern to him. Its skin was the mottled color of Lela's sunspots. I heard dad cough behind me.

"Aunt Lela, it's Jim. Remember me? This is my boy. I wrote that letter last week," dad mumbled, nervously wiping perspiration out of his eyes.

Lela didn't say anything. The silence was frightening. Her eyes were curtainless empty windows with an abandoned interior. I heard pole beans snapping between her fingers. Dad cleared his throat again. I wondered if she was deaf.

"Aunt Lela, did you get my letter?" dad asked, raising his voice.

Lela slowly turned her head to the screen door, shouting in Cuban. In a few seconds a dark-skinned boy materialized at the screen door. When he saw me he smiled. I smiled back. He looked a year or two older than me. Lela fired off another rapid stream of Cuban. He hurried down the steps, motioning me to follow him around the back. Later, when we went to the front of the house my dad was gone and Lela's rocking chair was empty.

My new friend's name was Roberto. He was a head taller than me and two years older. I liked him immediately. He had a friendly demeanor and a quick smile, sparkling white teeth and bright dark eyes. Lela was his grandmother. She had raised him since he was two years old, after her daughter ran off with an AWOL sailor.

We were standing in the front yard, a few feet from the sidewalk, the concrete buckling upward in protest at a banyan tree's aerial roots. The midday sun was baking the yard in its bright, white fury.

"We'd better go in. Lela will have dinner ready," Roberto said.
I thought it was odd to eat dinner in the middle of the day but I didn't say anything.

Inside the dark house the humid air was flavored by a pot of black beans cooking on a tiny gas stove. A thirteen inch black and white TV sat on top of a color console. Both had snowy, grainy pictures, their volume blasting. On one wall was a black velvet mural of Martin Luther King, John Kennedy and brother Robert, in profile.

Lela was slouched in a kitchen chair looking tired and defeated. One meaty arm wearily rested on the bare table, her other clutched her cane. The kitchen floor was cracked linoleum. With her cane she dragged a jagged piece of linoleum back to its matching hole.

The back of her cotton dress was drenched in perspiration, hanging sloppily off one shoulder. A dingy bra strap bit deeply into the padded flesh. She didn't hear us till Roberto spoke. She struggled around to us. Rivulets of sweat down both sides of her flushed face, she spoke to Roberto.

I followed Roberto through the musty house to the bathroom. The wood floor was tongue and groove pine worn smooth over the years by Lela's heavy step. In a bedroom I heard fan blades whirling.

Even in the small bathroom you couldn't escape Lela's scent in every corner. Her aging presence assaulted your senses. The lavatory was filled with tepid, greyish soap water. We washed our hands in it together. Roberto whispered that Lela only took a bath on Saturdays, preferring to sponge bath the rest of the week. The few hygiene essentials I saw were a sliver of soap, a hairbrush matted with Lela's white strands, a toothbrush in a jelly jar, and a rolled up tube of toothpaste. Hanging on a rusted cement nail, above the clawleg bathtub, was a red hot water bottle.

At the table I watched Lela laboriously stirring the beans while Roberto placed bowls, spoons, a loaf of Cuban bread, and a saucer of butter on the table. We ate quickly, listening to Lela smack her lips, chewing and swallowing. When she finished she plucked out her dentures, dropped them in a glass of baking soda, and waddled to her bedroom for her nap.

We heard Lela snoring in her bedroom as we quietly snuck out the screen door. There were three raspy snorts, a shuttering inhale, then a long gurgling exhale. Roberto said she would sleep two hours, wake up, and take her afternoon sponge bath.

Lela's husband built her cottage as an enticement to his proposal for marriage. They were married less than a year, Lela seven months pregnant with Roberto's mother when she stabbed her husband in the heart one night. She said it was an accident, she thought he was an intruder. The court ruled in her favor, but that didn't stop the townfolks from gossiping behind her back. She inherited the cottage and a decent bank account enabling her to raise her daughter without working or remarrying. Her neighbors never saw her grieving; life just went on. Her Conch heritage was as tough as the uncooked mollusc's meat.

We jumped off the porch and went to the side of the house. Roberto dropped to his knees and crawled into the cool darkness under the house then backed out with a mayonnaise jar in his hand.

"I want to show you something," he said, standing. Holes were punched in the metal lid of the jar. Tiny drops of condensation glistened, clinging to the glass. Squirming over a mat of decaying leaves were two huge, black scorpions. The biggest scorpion was wrestling with the other, trying to ride its back. Roberto held the jar up for inspection. Instinctively, I stepped back, repelled by their venomous appearance. The small scorpion kept twisting, trying to hook its barbed tail over its aggressor to sting it. But the bigger scorpion simply countered with its own tail to fend off the curving blow.

"The big one is a male," Roberto told me. "They're mating."

I watched the female try to squirm around with her forward pincers only to have the male use his advantageous weight to force her head down into the leaves.

"Looks like they're fighting to me," I said, fascinated.

"That's how they do it," he said.

"How long will that go on?" I asked. I felt sorry for the smaller, female scorpion.

"Not long," Roberto said, thumping the glass with his forefinger. Both scorpions froze. The male raised his curved stinger, the tiny hook poised, testing the air. The female tried to scramble from under him, but he was too quick and pinned her down.

"It looks like she doesn't like it," I said, watching her futile attempt to flee.

"They just act like that," Roberto said, flinching his brown shoulders.

"What are you going to do with them?" I asked.

"Watch them."

"Where did you get them?"

"I caught the female in the house. Under Lela's bed. The male I found outside."

"You ever been bit by one?"

"No. I know how to handle them. But Lela knew a man that was bit on the face while he was sleeping. She said his face and tongue swelled up so much he suffocated in his sleep," Roberto said.

"Just from one bite?" I asked, incredulously.

Roberto nodded his head. "Some people are allergic to them. Let's sit down and watch them. It's almost over."

We sat down in the backyard under the filtered shade of a poinciana tree, the mayonnaise jar with the dueling scorpions between us. For several minutes the female continued to struggle to escape from under the weight of the larger male scorpion. Suddenly, she abandoned her attempted flight, lowering herself rigidly to the glass floor, letting her aggressor subdue her. Her wicked, hooking tail went limp, her body no longer protesting the male's actions. A few more seconds passed, then the male seemed to relinquish the battle, letting the female scurry from under him. The male backed away against the glass and lay motionless. Ferociously, the female immediately charged the spent male, attacking him repeatedly with her stinger. It was the male's turn to be submissive, letting her strike him over and over without protest till he was defeated. His segmented body curled at the abdomen in a fetal position.

"What's she doing now?" I asked. Roberto held the jar up to his eyes.

"She killed him."

"Killed him? Why?"

"Now she will feed off his body while she waits to give birth to her offspring."

When Lela came out to the porch after her sponge bath, she still looked tired and haggard. She struggled with her cane to her rocking chair, collapsing with a shuddering sigh and leaned back to collect her breath. The afternoon sun was making its orange descent to the west. Two sailors stumbled by, heading to the docks. Their loud, slurred voices lowered to whispers when they noticed Lela glaring at them.

Lela withdrew a small change purse from between the cleavage of her watermelon breasts. Her shaking fingers handed us two quarters to get soft drinks from the deli down the street. We dashed off the porch, through the gate, and out to the sidewalk, leaving Lela to her senile rocking.

When we got back, Lela loomed larger than ever, rocking on her throne. We sat on the steps, our back to her, savoring every caramel sugared drop of our six ounce Cokes. I could smell the familiar sweet smell of rum and Lela's eyes seemed to have a shine on them. That's how every afternoon ended. The two of us, sitting on the steps sipping our Cokes, our backs softening the melancholy rhythm of Lela's rocking chair.

We checked on the pregnant scorpion every day. Over the weeks her belly swelled, while the dead male shriveled to a deflated carcass. When they were mating, I felt sorry for the female struggling under the male, but it was the male I felt sorry for now. He paid the ultimate sacrifice. Life for life. Procreation of the species. The needs of the many outweigh the needs of the few. I wondered if he knew what his fate was after satisfying his biological urge. How could he know? When he found out it was too late.

Several years later, dad told me Lela had died penniless in a nursing home. Roberto was busted for smuggling drugs and was facing thirty years in a federal prison. Lela put her house up for bond and lost it to the state when Roberto jumped bail and disappeared. That was when her house was put up for sale and Lela was taken to a nursing home. She shunned her will to live and died peacefully in her sleep a month later.

Three days before dad showed up one evening with two Greyhound bus tickets back home, Roberto hurried me around to the back of the house to watch the mother scorpion deliver her young into the world. We knew it was going to happen any day when she stopped eating and seemed to remain in one place.

We watched in amazement as the tiny, light brown scorpions started emerging from under the mother's abdomen. Frantically, the siblings swarmed over each other and their docile mother, searching for nourishment and salvation in the world they were thrust into. In horror, I watched the tiny scorpions attack their placid parent. Repeatedly striking her with their poisonous tails in a frenzied, cannibalistic orgy, they eventually pushed her over on her back and devoured her soft underbelly. Never once did she raise her tail to defend herself, instead accepting her role as the first and last provider to her children.

# THE HUNDRED-DOLLAR KITTY CAT

## ROSALIND BRACKENBURY

The cat from Pepe's had been missing since Tuesday. Someone had pinned a handwritten notice on the telephone poles around town: missing, black kitty cat, 100 dollars reward. Key West was full of them - missing animals, notices on telephone poles on street corners, large cash rewards. But this was the biggest reward. The cat in the xeroxed photograph looked heavily male and predatory, with wide-apart black ears. Not really a kitty cat at all.

Jack thought, you could do good business, just before Christmas, with this losing and finding of costly pets. He wasn't surprised when he met the cat in question creeping about his own back yard as if it were in a real jungle. It was a sleek black tomcat, its glance wolfish.

"Kitty, kitty-cat!" he called. Wide jade eyes outstared him. The cat hissed and ran. He caught it with both hands, between two of the old armchairs that furnished his yard and held it down on the gravel. He picked it up from above, his hands full of fur and muscle, dangled it and dropped it into the house. The cat ran and hid under the couch, where he couldn't reach it. He went immediately to Pepe's to ask about the prize, and a blank young woman at the bar said she knew nothing about money but sure, the cat was gone. When Jack went back to his own place, there was no sign of the damn kitty-cat anywhere, even in the narrow darkness under the couch. He pushed it back and found an old checkbook and some overdue bills, instead.

The back yard was suddenly full of people. There was Annie and Cheryl their grand-daughter, and Paul from across the street, and another young guy he didn't know, and they were all drinking coffee. It was a late warm morning, the day before Christmas Eve. There'd been the debris of Christmas preparations around for days, cookies made by his grand-daughters crumbling in the kitchen, nutshells and cut-up colored paper all over the front step. Square packages blocked his way wherever he stepped. The evidence of Christmas was all around them in tight-wrapped holly-berried snow-blobbed rectangles that looked as though they'd come from a million miles from Florida. In the cage in the back yard was the kitty-cat, its sad little rasp of a tom-cat voice lifting to punctuate the talk with sudden hoarse cries.

Paul was talking. He said, "Well, when we had our dogs in kennels up in Minnesota we used to go in at night and liberate them. We used to wear black, with masks, and go in through the doggy doors. They'd cost far more than we could afford, it was the only way. Of course, we'd had a few drinks first."

Annie said, "Would you believe it, a hundred bucks for an animal?"

Then she said, "D'you know, my cat died when I took it into kennels? They actually killed my cat? And of course, you miss a cat. Any pet, you miss."

Cheryl said, "I wish I had one."

"What, honey?"

"A pet. A cat. Or maybe I'd prefer a dog."

Cheryl, who was only eleven, lived in a house crammed with babies. Jack thought she had the look sometimes of a strained young mother, dark rings under her eyes, a restless anxious searching look about her, and it pained him to see it. Now, she studied the kitty-cat and the caged tom stared back.

"Dad won't let me have one."

"Your house is too full already," said her grandmother. Annie loved the little girls, the exhausted little band that followed Cheryl around. She would have loved for them to have a country childhood, animals, the sorcery of trees. But Clem thought animals around the place were too much of a good thing when you had as many female children as he did.

"Go get another coffee mug for your grandpa, Cheryl," she said.

"Mug or cup?" Cheryl liked cups with matching saucers, silverware, things they didn't have much in her house. She went with her grandmother to endless yard sales, both of them looking for treasure. Jack thought, if you raise a kid in a town built on booty and wreckers' gold, what can you expect.

"Oh, cup, mug, anything you like, sweetheart. Just something to put coffee in."

Cheryl went on her new long legs like a racehorse colt. Paul was lighting a cigarette, blowing out smoke.

"And when they said a hundred dollars, a HUNDRED, just for having dogs in a kennel, imagine, my wife used to stick her boobs out so they looked like missile cones and point them straight at the guy so he couldn't think. A hundred, you must be joking. And the guy would flinch. He was scared to death of her, with those boobs. I used to make her put on a push-up bra to go see people like that. Him and the tax-man, the gas-man, anyone we owed money to."

Cheryl began to giggle. Sometimes she just loved adults' conversations, the way they could say anything and not get told to behave. The kitty-cat in the cage stuck one black leg in the air and began to wash his ass with his tongue. Everything seemed funny, suddenly - everything.

"Which reminds me," said Paul their neighbour, "Why the nasty tits today, Annie?"

"What d'you mean? It's my new push-up bra. I bought it specially for Christmas. It's supposed to drive Jack wild."

"Do me a favour and go bra-less for Christmas, will you? You look terrifying like that."

"I spent a hundred bucks on new bras last week, I'm not going to not wear them."

"They terrify me," said Paul.

Cheryl went on giggling, loving it, shooting her round black eyes from one of them to the other.

"A hundred bucks on bras?" said Jack. "Sure. Why not?"

Paul said, "They terrify me. They terrified the guy at the kennels and the tax-man and the gas-man and they terrify me. Those guys had to put a counter between them and my ex-wife."

Annie said, "We all know why that was."

Cheryl snorted with her new, nearly-teenage laughter. She laughed because she was in it now, the rude jokes, the bra stories, the silliness they enjoyed. It was because on the bra-buying expedition to J.C. Penney, her grandma had bought her one too, her first small bra, and she wore it now like a prize under her T-shirt. A breast now grew safely in each cup of it, like a seedling in a flower pot. Her Dad had not wanted her to have one, saying it wasn't necessary, women didn't wear them any more, and what an extravagance. But Cheryl knew that real women, like her grandma, did. She knew it was for something else, that wasn't necessity. She needed one so that she could sit there and understand the jokes and feel adult and safe at last. She longed for more now, for the intoxicating mixed-up sound of what adults talked about when they were alone.

Paul said, "I don't need any more therapy, Annie, I went through all that with my ex-wife."

"And look where it got you!"

"Exactly."

Cheryl thought that perhaps it was being terrified of bras that made Paul live alone in a trailer in the park across the street. Perhaps her father was terrified of them too, perhaps that was why he was angry when she came back from the shopping trip with her grandma. How strange things were. She let out an explosion of mirth and fear. Just think, being terrified of a bra!

"What about that kitty-cat, grandpa?" said Annie, changing the tone.

Jack looked at the cat. What on earth did all this conversation have to do with anything?

"Well, are you going to take it back to Pepe's and get the reward?"

"Sure. Soon as anyone's there that'll hand over the money. Is there any food we can feed him? Poor devil's bound to be starving by now."

The cat, tired with captivity, lay like a pool of shadow at the bottom of the cage. He closed his eyes to very narrow slits, the way cats do in extremes of pleasure or boredom.

"I'll get him some milk. Can I get him some milk, grandma?"

"Cat that size'll want more than milk."

Overhead the sky darkened between the mango leaves. It would rain soon. The clouds stirred and sudden wind blew a huge leaf down and carried it to the table like a green plate.

"Look!" Cheryl exclaimed. She put it on her head, a wide green mango hat. She felt cute, excited, stirred by something she couldn't yet recognise.

Suddenly she saw it, the connection between all these things. That was what being adult meant, it was seeing what connected with what. She sat up, elbows on knees, her hair coming out from under the leaf-hat. Up there, thunder moved and groaned and the first fat drops fell from the sky.

"I know," she said, "Grandpa can take the kitty-cat back and get a hundred dollars and then Grandma and I can get a hundred dollars' worth of bras and then we can terrify EVERYBODY just like Paul said."

"Don't talk nonsense," her grandma said. Cheryl thought this wasn't fair as they all talked such nonsense themselves. She looked at her grandfather, her chin up.

Jack saw her grin and her flashing eyes. He felt afraid, but it was like being afraid of the thunder or the rain, it was for something you couldn't do anything about.

They hurried the coffee things indoors as the drops fell faster.

"Come on, Cheryl," Jack said, "Time to take the kitty-cat back and claim our reward, before it's too late."

"Too late for what, grandpa?"

"Just that you shouldn't leave things," he said. "You shouldn't ever leave things too late."

His grand-daughter walked down the street beside him and he wanted to protect her childish beauty from all eyes. She skipped a pace or two. She was still a baby really. There was just the troubled adult look she had sometimes, as though she was responsible for all the problems of the world. That tiredness in her glance, as if sometimes it was all too much. And now this this talk. He didn't know what had disturbed him today, but something had.

"What you going to do with that cat, Jack?" People asked him now, looking at the angry animal in the cage in the yard.

"Take it back, soon as someone'll give me the hundred bucks."

At the bar, the same bored young woman was filling in for the holidays.

"You'll have to wait till Tony comes in. I don't know nothin' about no reward."

The cat glared at him, its green eyes pale jade like the Back Country water in summer. It would not be petted or fed with milk.

Only when he put in a handful of fresh squid, did it eat, with a feral shake of its broad head as its jaws worked on the squid. It was there all through Christmas, eating squid and ballyhoo. It stared out at them as they drank their coffee and wine, out in the yard, under the mango tree.

Then on the morning of the day after Christmas, he went out sleepy and half-dressed into the yard with a coffee-mug in his hand and saw that it was gone. The cage door was open. His first feeling was of relief. It wasn't right to have an animal locked up as if it were a criminal, especially not at Christmas. He sat down on a broken wicker chair and examined the open cage. The cat had messed in one corner and there were still fragments of fish bones in another. It had tried to eat as far away as possible from where it had made its mess. Cats minded about that, about privacy and neatness. They dug holes and squatted trembling and covered it all up afterwards.

Cheryl came into the yard through the back gate, with her small twin sisters, one held tightly by each hand. Their Dad had dropped them off, she said. He wanted to go back to sleep.

"Cheryl, baby, know anything about the kitty-cat?"

"No grandpa."

"He's just gone. Can't imagine how."

"No grandpa."

But he knew from her face that she did know.

"You sure, honey?"

"Mmm. Grandpa, you kept him in the cage too long. You said you shouldn't leave things too late."

"So I did, too. So what did you do with him?"

"I just let him out, grandpa. He just went right back down the street home. He just knew right where to go. He just wanted to go home."

"Oh, I see. Well, you probably did right, honey." Cheryl pushed back her heavy dark brown hair and looked at him with her adult, peering look.

"Are you angry, grandpa?'

'Hell, no, baby. Anybody's got a right to go home at Christmas, wouldn't you say? Even a goddamn kitty-cat."

"What about the hundred bucks, though?"

"Well, a hundred bucks is just a hundred bucks. You thought he oughta go home, he oughta go home."

"But what about the bras, grandpa?"

"Bras, what bras?"

"Grandma's, mine. The ones that scare people."

"Honey, that's just a manner of speaking, it don't mean a thing. Hell, you women don't have to pay me back for no bras. You have what makes you happy."

"But grandma said it'd drive you wild."

"Well, that wasn't exactly what she meant."

"What did she mean, then?"

"Something you'll get to understand when you're older. Now don't you worry about it."

"But I am older, now."

"You're not that old, sweetheart. Now just you quit worrying and go play. I'll watch the twins."

He felt benevolent, at peace. The anxiety had faded from her face.

The next time he walked down the street past Pepe's he saw the big black cat sitting only just inside the door in a triangular patch of sun, licking its lips. It stared at him with slitty, satisfied eyes. It stretched a black leg like a cut of ham in the warmth of the winter sun and he saw its furry black balls like two eggs in a pouch.

Hell no, that ain't no kitty-cat, that's a wild animal, that is, home for just as long as it chooses to be. It had gone to his place of its own accord and gone home as soon as Cheryl had let it out, doing what it damn' well pleased, as it always would. It had jumped bail, the hundred-dollar kitty-cat, it wasn't going to be anybody's Christmas prize. Good luck to it, it was the way things should be. And the way she had grinned at him, his blackeyed girl in her wildness and innocence, was worth more than a hundred bucks to him, anytime.

# BLUE MENACE

## *THERESA FOLEY*

The silver bottlenosed dolphin cut through the crystal blue water off the long strand of islands known as the Florida Keys. Ahead swam a pod of a dozen of the mammals, and he raced toward them effortlessly. He was built for speed, motion, a charioteer of the sea. Larger than the others by several feet, the majestic old male took a jagged path around the smaller dolphins, as if to slip under their monitoring mechanism of sonar.

He circled twice, hanging back, clicking now, audible and distinct from the sounds of the group. He waited for his own sonar to bounce back to create the hologram in his brain. When it did, he could see them in three dimensions, the shadows of their curved bodies, their muscles, he could even see his own shape approaching the cluster they'd formed. He examined the image until he spotted her, a mature female nearly as muscular as he. The big grey calculated her position and the distance, then swam forward again to reach her. He wasted little time before brushing up against her a few times, then inserting himself into her pale body. They swam together, warm Gulf water sliding over their sleek bodies, washing over a ritual that dated back 65 million years.

Separating, the silver male swam alone again. From the point of his nose to his wide graceful flukes, he was twice the length of a man. He steered with two tapered flippers, boned appendages that have five curious fingers almost like a human's. His dorsal fin, made of soft tissue, was darker grey and swept away from his body with hydrodynamic grace. He circled the pod, imaging them again, this time selecting a smaller female. He repeated the brief courtship, rubbing up against her to indicate interest and then slipping into her with a rough shove to move together through the blue stream. Dolphins are not naturally monogamous, and the old grey felt a deep contentment in taking his pleasure, obeying his instincts, as his ancestors had over the ages. Locked with the small female, his body waved in soft rhythm until he

29

broke off and moved away.

Then he flipped the powerful flukes and put a few hundred yards of sparkling sea between himself and the pod. The other males were watching him closely, their clicking and high pitched song sounding more frantic now. Finally they organized into a line of defense, swimming into protective position around their wards. The older males, the guardians, had been willing to tolerate the silver's philandering once, but his advances were too aggressive for a wanderer who simply wanted to join the pod. This old one was not interested in socializing. He was a loner.

The group moved along through the turquoise sea at top speed, leaving the big grey behind. The dolphins headed to the cove where they rested each afternoon after feeding. Once they reached the protected half-moon shaped bay, they dropped their guard, spreading out again. The younger animals frolicked, breaking the surface of the ocean in joyful leaps, the antics that endear the species so well to humankind.

Near the place where the cove spilled out into the open sea, a two-year-old swam slowly alone. She was small with velvet skin the color of mercury. She played, rolling like a barrel, the warm water near the surface caressing her skin. Her solo aquabatic performance seemed as perfectly engineered as a glider dancing in the clouds on a windy day.

She rose to the surface to draw a breath of air through the blowhole behind her head when the grey approached hard and fast from the side. He pushed against her, then down, down, pressing to submerge her toward the sandy bottom. The old male rubbed his left side against her softness. She tried to move, to twist away, but couldn't. One eye saw him, huge and urgent, ready for her. Compared to the others, her suitor was a giant and he had a fierceness about him that she had not seen in the others. She tried to move away, to get back to the pod but he was on her like they'd been glued together.

As she lifted her tailfin up, ready to make one more try to evade the big grey, she felt him slide, large and rough, into her. She yielded and a natural movement began, turning violent as the big grey began shaking. She fell into his rhythm, no longer seeking escape, to join the others. Together they moved to the south, toward the open water, to the deep, the water around them seeming as infinite as the power in their bodies. She sensed a violence in this one that was foreign. In all her learning, the dolphin ways had been gentle and loving. She'd never felt the urgency and pain the big grey sent into her as they coupled.

Panic set into her heart. She wanted to return to her family now, but she was helpless as he swam with her, pushing her to the south, to the big island, the place of magic. The island had fewer boats, fewer humans, fewer dolphins in fact, and the secret guarded place. She couldn't go with him, wouldn't.

As he rubbed roughly, she turned her eye toward him and saw the thick white scars on the sides of his head and further down by his flippers. Telltale markings of human captivity. In an instant, an image of thick black nylon straps holding a human-made box onto a dolphin shape seared her mind, and then the image and the big grey were gone. She was alone now, shaken up but free to find the cove, the pod, her mother, back to safety.

# COME WITH US NOW

## *JUDY ADAMS*

Felina is a healer in Key West. Her husband of many years is named Zorro. They are one of the few really married couples in old town. They talk of love and peace more than most of us do. Whatever you are interested in at any particular time, they are able to integrate their message into the discussion. Are you into yogurt? So are they, and glad to explain how to culture your yogurt in love and give it more power, the better to nourish you with. Felina understands all about vibrations, she feels them and sends them. Zorro likes to eat yogurt.

Are you sewing for the season? Felina hates to wear clothes herself; in fact, you must come to the house to visit without clothes as they interfere with the flow between people. If you must be dressed in public, and even in Key West that is still so, she knows just the right colors to transmit love, excitement, joy, peace, and success. A person can definitely affect everything happening about him or her just by the color of the clothing. Nothing to take lightly. However, it is always better to leave the body uncovered to the sunlight, moonlight, candlelight, or naked 40 watt bulb. Felina has studied from a master who came to town and had a seminar on color at the health food store. Zorro loves to see naked bodies in the light. He is very much affected by the light. Naked bodies he looks closely at, just to see if they affect him, and really, they don't. Felina will assure you that Zorro is not at all affected sexually by a nude body. Sex is not their bag, but the absorption of light is.

Are you into music, the dulcimer, the guitar, flute, dancing? Felina understands the language of music, how it lifts men from the mortal dust and lifts, lifts, lifts us out of the top of the head, projecting the music maker, the dancer into a cosmic embrace with universality, unity and harmony; transmutes, transcends, positively charges the polarity of a room full of people. Zorro loves to watch the ladies in the flashing lights of the Boat Bar and has bought Felina a g-string and rhinestone pasties to give her during the full of the moon. Yin and yang, they weave through any conversation; all the while Felina looks deeply into the eyes she is speaking to, while Zorro stands next to the corpus, rubbing and squeezing, now the arm, now the knee.

They have come to the small apartment of Jasmine, to visit. They love her so much, she is so beautiful. Her spirit, her dancing under black lights, and the very brief clothing she wears about town, chosen to reveal while covering a very voluptuous body. A body vibrant, young, supple, firm, and warm with the pulse of trust and life. She just loves to commune with Felina, she is so spiritual, open, experienced and approving. A new friend, Michael, has followed the group to Jasmine's from sunset. Felina is going to share her secret of astral projection with him. He is very interested in getting as far away from his body as possible right now. He has just quit smoking and lost his old lady of six months. Somehow, he has a hang up and Felina says she knows she can help him. Michael, six foot four of solid muscle gained from military training and heavy work, is probably muscle bound, and Felina knows how to release the tension of these muscles — to help the bronze youth let go of his corrupt body and search the universe in his astral form. She can feel it all about him, clinging to his full muscles, thick curly hair, slim hips, and who knows where else? She knows how to release the astral body, detach it from his furry chest and firm solar plexus. Jasmine, too, is interested in mind travel, and is happy to have them eating her food for the week and finishing the juices. She drinks a beer. Felina and Zorro do not touch drugs. They have a natural high. Both the young people would like to have a natural high. Christ, the price of gold is ridiculous.

Zorro sits on the couch eating, first the cheese, then the cookies, and now the fruit. The mango is too much work. The cherries are so small. He eats a banana, then peaches. The food is gone, his eyes close and close, his head drops to his chest, and he jerks awake with a start.

"See," Felina says, "Zorro has just returned to his body, that is why he started, jumped sort of. He goes into a trance so easily. With training, anyone can project the astral body. See, there goes Zorro again."

Jasmine removes the dishes from the floor so that Michael can stretch full length. "Gee, I wish we had a tape recorder so we could get all of this. Maybe next time."

Felina, on her knees beside her waiting pupil, extends her middle fingers.

"These are the axis, the power transmitters. If I run out of power, Jasmine, you must give me yours and if we need more, Zorro will transmit his to you and then through me to Michael. The right hand is the positive, the left negative, unless of course you are left-handed. I will draw out with the left and transmit with the right. Here make a pyramid with your fingers, to trap and hold power. Here, like this."

Taking his fingers, they form a triangle with the thumbs and index fingers. Felina runs her finger up Michael's very luxuriant midline of hair, always upward, always stroking upward.

"If you must, you must move the fingers apart, like this, down again." Fingers spread along the dark hair. "Oh, Michael, I feel your astral body. Let me touch it and you concentrate. Can you feel my vibrations?" Slowly she passes her hands over the prone man, breathing deeply to relax and concentrate. All over his body she glides hands, all the while looking deeply into his eyes, so blue with such long lashes.

"Do you feel anything?"

"No! I don't."

"I do, but I am really relaxed and enjoying this."

"You can feel it?"

"Yes, it is hard and pulsing."

She touches his groin, through the cut off jeans.

"You are firmly attached here. Hard for you to let go?" Hands up to his head and through his hair.

"You're a very sensitive person, your astral self is very large about your head. A high intelligence, and much knowledge of life in one so young. You're an old soul. Your capacity to love is limitless and you will gain in power and never be diminished by age. Very spiritual, Michael. Never have I felt such a big strong astral head. Oh this is so exciting. You excite me very much. When you get loose finally, you are going to zoom off like a rocket and you will find fulfillment and release."

"Really?"

"Yes, and I will help you, even if it takes all night."

Leaving off massage of his astral self she lays her hand upon his genitals.

"This is the first chakra, and all life flows from it. Its color is red. Do you feel the heat of my hands?"

"I feel something."

"My hands are burning. The color is red and the food to feed this chakra is also red. I will line up your polarities before I explain more."

"You know, this is new to me."

"I have been studying a lot and took the class. Now I have a master, but be patient, I am learning."

Placing her left finger on the top of his head and the right on his tail bone, she says, "This is the way to line up your polarity. You, of course, are lying always head to the south. Do you feel the power?"

No answer.

"I do. I feel myself flowing into you, and when your polarity is just right, you rock it like this as you would to soothe, to give comfort, as a mother rocks a child. Do you feel anything? You have to be kidding. I feel a great power. Are you receiving it? Is it like an electric shock?"

"More like a throb. Heat definitely. I can really feel the heat."

"Don't fight it. Let it spread to your toes and to the top of your head. Let me show you your chakras and then I will line your polarity while you lie on your back."

"OK, I remember the first one, but you can show me again. Maybe I remember wrong. I want to get it right."

"Of course."

Her hand again on his genitals. "This is the first chakra, all life flows from it and its color is red and it is nourished and will grow if fed foods that are red. You are a meat eater aren't you, Michael? I certainly thought so."

Moving the hands to his stomach, slowly. "This is the second chakra. Its color is orange and it is fed with orange foods. It is the home of what is lowest in man. Your astral body is not at all connected here, this is just wonderful. And here, your solar plexus, is the third chakra. Its color is yellow. It needs yellow foods and sunlight. That is why you must be naked in the sun whenever possible. It is the seat of power. This on your chest is the fourth chakra. Its color is green, and from here comes your growth, of the body and spirit, powered from your lungs and heart. And the fifth chakra is in your throat and the back of the neck. Its color is blue and you feed it blue foods. What foods are blue? Grapes, you know, wine."

"Oh, drink wine, wine, fruit of the vine?"

"Yes, I think so. And here in the middle of your forehead is your third eye."

"My what? I've never heard of that."

"I have," says Jasmine. "It is what we call the 'mind's eye' sometimes."

"OK, I gotcha."

"You are right, of course, Jasmine. Once we all had an eye here, but as man became more physical, it atrophied and all that remains to us now is the inner sense, which we must use to seek enlightenment, so the man of the future, whom we are going to be reincarnated as, will also have it. The color is purple. What do we eat purple to feed it? I think color alone, as in flowers and wearing purple clothes, is our food for the sixth chakra. And here at the top, where your soft spot is — do you still have it? — is the seventh chakra. Here your astral body escapes, as does the soul when you die. The Hopis call it keeping the top of the head open. Its color is aquamarine and we all know the next color is ultraviolet, which we cannot see."

"Can you see my aura?"

"No, but I can see with my third eye and my seventh chakra that you have many bodies surrounding the astral. First the aura, then your body of vibrations, then your electrical body."

By this time Felina has raised her hands quite far above Michael's body, caressing his electrical body as her watermelon breasts, very full, caress his face.

"Do you remember any of your former lives?"

"I try and try and can only get as far as my mother's womb and hearing her scream 'I don't want this thing growing in me!'"

"But you know, you picked your mother? You have probably been related in many incarnations. Perhaps you have even been her mother. We go through eternity reuniting and working toward God and unity with consciousness we have always known."

"Why would we pick the same ones?"

"I can remember just faintly, and not very often, I was a priestess in the temple of Venus," offers Jasmine.

"That is why you dress the way that you do. You can show the rest of us how to enjoy and express sexuality."

"Maybe that is it. Felina, I think you could be right. What do you remember?"

"Roll over, Michael, and I will align your polarity from the spine. I have been a healer many times, I feel this."

"How am I going to make a pyramid while I lie on my stomach?"

"I will place your head between two pillows so you can breathe. Zorro, hand me those pillows from the couch."

Zorro, back from his astral wanderings, hands the pillows and pours another glass of juice, which he finishes in three swallows.

"Do you have any candy or nuts?"

"Gee, I am sorry. How about more fruit?"

Felina places her finger on the top of Michael's head and stretches herself along his back to reach his coccyx with her other hand.

"You can put your hand in my jeans. I want to feel a real connection." He loosens his belt and unbuttons the top of his pants, exposing his buttocks, just the tops. Zorro stops eating the fruit and moves to align his polaris, watching the buttocks closely. So closely. He shifts around on the couch, not able to find a comfortable position for his condition. Felina, her positive and negative sensors firmly holding Michael's tail bone and head now says, "And just like before, the polarity is rocked gently back and forth, smoothly, gently, like this. Do you feel the vibrations? Oh, your body is not lined up correctly, move around this way."

Zorro, with agility, moves facing the same direction, exactly, totally, to judge the focus of his eyes and tense concentration. Felina rocks the long body.

"Would you like a massage? We can teach you and then you can massage us. We will correct you as you learn. A proper massage will free your astral body and you may go anywhere in the universe — to the past, to other planes, to the future. There is no limit."

"I don't know if I can keep this on a spiritual level."

"You can. We massage and are massaged by many, always detached from the sexual. To touch another body is only sexual if the consciousness can go no higher, which it can with practice, of course. Zorro has complete massages, I mean complete, any part, any length of time, and never gets excited. Two girls massaged him yesterday and you didn't get at all excited, did you dear?"

"It sure felt good."

"I bet it did! Let me put it to you this way: I'd love a massage, and I would love to leave my body, and I would just love for you to knock yourself out massaging me and I promise never to get excited, if that would offend you." His voice breaks and he blurts, "I don't want to, but I know if you massage my balls, I will get excited."

"Oh Michael, with your strong mental power, I know we can teach you to enjoy complete total release without ever being aroused. Can't we, Zorro?"

"If anybody can, it is Felina."

"My power will enter you and heal you. You will lose your desire, awaken all of your chakras and be united with your destiny in white purity."

"Like I say, I am inexperienced with being touched all over and not getting excited, so if you want to try and just leave out a few parts, I want to go ahead."

"What do you say, Zorro?"

"If anybody can teach him, we can."

"Do you want to try?"

"We will both work on you, and Jasmine can help, too, by transmitting her power through Zorro, if you would like to, Jasmine. Do you have a massage table? We really need to be up off the floor."

"Oh, we can skip it and I'll make something up and invite you over then."

"We have so much energy here tonight. I hate to waste all the energy. Do you feel all the energy? It is cosmic."

Rubbing her hands together, Felina extends her arms and says, "Can you feel all the electricity shooting from my fingertips?"

Peering closely, Michael says, "No."

Again she rubs her hands together and touches him.

"That felt like a jolt. I guess someday I will be able to see more. I am trying to get free. I really am."

"How about we use the bed? That will elevate you and we can all work on you?"

"I have a waterbed. It is not much like a massage table. We would still be on the same level, like we are now."

"Zorro, I think we should be up off of the floor, don't you agree? Oh yes, that will lift us all to the spiritual plane. Let's all get in the bed. Take off your clothes so the power can flow unbroken."

# THE PLACE WE LIVE

### ROBIN ORLANDI

Chugging out the Northwest channel at dusk,
around midnight we have moored off Cottrell Key
the houseboat rocks in the rhythms of our Mother's arms,
we are blanketed with stars, the bright sting of the Scorpion,
and a full Dipper tilting earthward,
we lay on our backs as children peering into the universe.

This is the place we live.

The sharp slapping of fin flesh on water wakes us,
invisible leaping and roiling out there in the darkness,
airborne rays or flying fish, some alarmed prey
defying the tightening links of the food chain.
Slap, splash! slap, splash!
a chorus of scales against the sea
waves glittering etched with moonlight
we gaze across dumbfounded
and find ourselves tiny as grains of sand swept within
this infinity of air and water that sustains us.

This is the place we live.

We fall asleep on the roof,
the full brilliant moon drilling our eyelids,
wind from the north rips over the waves
all night roaring savage lullabies into uncovered ears
and all night we awake to watch the constellations
wander westward chased by dawn,
the whole heaven swinging to and fro
rocks the cradle.

# The Place We Live

This is the place we live.

Solar winds driving the dawn
drive cold night from our mammal skins.
A kettle of vultures wheel over nearby mangroves,
but among them, one borne distinct from the rest,
twice the size, white head unmistakable,
vast wingspan a black crescent moon rising
steady he hovers higher, effortless yet all powerful
Bald Eagle surveys this country whose spirit
has been captured in his crooked claws -
endangered species, broken eggshells, dead chicks, icon of America,
legislation, protection, comeback, comeback, comeback —
The wings' trailing edges ripple like prairie grass,
those amber waves of grain across America's slowly eroding heartland.

Eagle, drive open these eyes to see
straight through the New World Disorder,
the corporate morgues and caskets of dollars
bearing our Mother's body,
let all people see with your blazing yellow eyes the other lives
clustered beneath your furious survival,
your furious wings beating against extinction:
the cormorants and mergansers full of selenium,
the Florida Panthers' crooked offspring muted with mercury,
the glorious corals choking to blackbanded skeletons,
the seacow and sea turtle prop scarred,
great singing whales entangled in driftnet and sickened in a poisonous ocean
and all the rest carry upon your mighty wingbeats
flying straight off the cursed dollar bill
and back into the wild heart of creation
where beats our common blood.
Carry this message
Our work is nowhere near done,
our work is barely just begun,
to save this, the place in which we live.

A test for the place we live:
    Name the soil below us.
-Miami and Key Largo limestones, respectively oolitic and coralline.
    Where does our drinking water come from?
-Navy Wells on the mainland, drawn from the Biscayne Aquifer,
pumped through one hundred and sixty plus miles of PVC pipeline.
-Or from the once freshwater lens beneath Key West,
steeped in formaldehyde from the cemetery,
dosed with trickled down DDT from the Army-Navy,
saline infiltrated and seeded
with injected unmentionable bacteria and stormwater runoff,
all of which any politician in his deep pockets categorically denies.
    Name three edible native species.
-Conch, custard apple, guava.
    Name three endangered native species.
-Key Deer, Stock Island Snail, Key Largo Woodrat.
    From where you stand, point north.
    How many days until the next full moon?
    Where does your sewage go?
-Key West Wastewater Plant on Fleming Key for secondary treatment,
no nutrient stripping, processed effluent pumped
directly offshore, next to the ship channel.
-Or to a neighborhood package treatment plant,
raw waste mixed with chlorine, stirred and dumped
right there, in my bay, your canal and
speaking for heron, egret, kingfisher, osprey,
our estuary, thank you very much!

-Or underground, raw, into septic tanks, or cesspits which fail,
or down shallow injection wells where,
aided by the churning of the waves
effluent migrates through porous rocks
and in hours or a few days resurfaces in my canal,
your bay or speaking for fish, bird, coral, turtle,
and marine mammals everywhere,
our ocean, thank you very much!

# The Place We Live

This is the place we live.

On the houseboat,
morning broken over us we prepare to dive
and all the daylight details burst pulsing through these human eyes:
Nurseshark, barracuda, spiny lobster, eel grass,
gorgonians, elkhorn, staghorn, finger, star and
brain corals, sandflats, flamingo tongues, sea urchins,
anemones, tophats, angelfish, parrotfish, triggerfish,
hog snapper, grouper, yellowtail, frigatebird,
osprey, pelican, egret, heron, man o'war, sea cucumber, phytoplankton.
This great web of being wheels above and below us
floating on the living sea we are woven within the waves and come clean,
baptized back into our animal nature of skin and blood, flesh and fin
eye to shining eye within the breathing of the tides and weaving of the stars
This is the place,
this is the place,
this is the place
we all live
praise it.

# ISLAND OF BONES

## *J.T. EGGERS*

She does not have to think. She does not have to see. She does not have to remember, yet she tries in earnest to listen. She wants to understand. Voices no longer clamor from the outside but there are still plenty, mocking, from within.

Here at the end of the road she hears sound differently. Palms rustle in the night and sound like lonely rain. Sticky men breathe and drool. "Don't worry, I'm not going to rape you." Her dress tears. Sound bleeds into her ears, all thick and dull and slow like the air on which it rides. Things here take time, like to live takes time, and for her, here at the end of the road, time has all but run out.

Ever so slowly an echo rises up from her bombed out inner blackness, a sort of psychotic hiccup she gets between drinks. This is a glitch to which she is accustomed; there is no new music. Today, though, the chord is struck in a different key. It comes brightly and with a new appeal, a certain sharpness and unexpected luster it has lacked before. This echo is, at first, nothing but a faint whisper. A suggestion, a spark, a word, nothing more: "Jump."

Soon the echo becomes louder, cajoling, smartly reasoning that the thud of her head against the ground is the only thing that could save her now. It is the only thing left; redemption at last.

She fights her opponent blindfolded, wounding herself with the sharp daggers she has honed from her remaindered emotion. When the pain becomes too great, when she twists those little knives and their steely points are well dug in, simply trying to listen becomes somehow too hard. Then she pays for and prays for bottled blanket darkness to remove her and comfort her; to protect her from her sins.

The money always appears. It just comes out of nowhere, from no one. She is not civilized, she is Cayo Hueso: alone, an island of bones, hot, high, and dirty, choking from overuse.

Coming full on too early and staying much too late destroyed her illusion of tanned tropical goodness, so today like some shark she must move or die. She dives straight down and deep, cutting through the old island streets in circles, pausing only to make urgent phone calls to no one, to blather and to plead with an unyielding dial tone. As she passes through the day she ignores sunshine and music and tourists' pointed passings in favor of an invisible sound's tricky company. The sound of the echo: "Jump."

By night she is ignored, and this she can comprehend, for they would see too much if they saw her, if they really saw her. It is much safer for people to pretend that her ugliness does not exist or disgust. They must blind themselves to it, this girl on her island, this collision of the beautiful and the grotesque. It is an ugly, maiming mess best not seen by clean young America.

Her life is not golden color in a warm sunset sky but all mixed up and muddled, the poetic insanity and poisoned delight of an oil slick rainbow amoeba in the Gulf. She is the bird with tar on its feathers. She is the turtle with a plastic baggie and six-pack rings in its stomach. She is starving.

On her back in his bedroom she catches glimpses of a blue-black sky through a tiny window up high in the eaves. All color looks polarized as time stands still and that brilliant blue-black is momentarily obscured by the rhythmic bobbing of coarse brown hair and bronzed neck. What is his name?

She can see a lone palm tree that looks quite flat and that is exactly the way she feels as she drifts in and out of consciousness, as he drifts in and out of her. How long does this take? Time is another mystery, as her haze changes moment to hour, hour to eternity. Sometimes she pretends that she isn't there at all. She thinks this might be a dream; perhaps he is her prince, or someone who really cares.

When he says "make love" she wants too much to believe. "Make love one more time." Love the come as it drips down her leg and she wishes for a tissue. Love the back-aching bowleggedness of time given in the back of a brown Monte Carlo. Love the hot kiss in a cool barroom while his wife holds dinner at home. No suede-soft, untouchable, knowing love for her. She deserves only the kind with legs splayed, head hitting, and back up hard against concrete block.

Raw sex perfume fills the room and settles onto her soul a musty, musky film. She reeks, and listens for the scent of love. Certainly she would jump at any chance to have it, clean and sweet like her most sacred childhood wishes.

When he is finally spent he snores. She showers, scrubbing herself raw. What can she do with this clammy smell? The water is as hot as it will get; it is hotter than she can stand. No amount of soap will rinse away the remorse that has worked itself deep beneath her skin to gnaw at her bones. Such agony has dulled her complexion, made her sallow and weary.

She dries herself with his towel, surveying the latest in a wide array of burns, splotches, and marks that will soon become blistered and purple.

Though it is not safe she emerges from her daze. It is not her choice to be thrust into this rare moment of clarity. She grasps at the horror and the truth of her dirty condition. Retching in fear and in sickness, she can do nothing but watch ghastly shadows on the wall and hope for her heart to stop. She listens to the insidious echo welling its one way word up from the pit: "Jump."

When she is able, when it is dark enough again, she grabs her tattered dress and tries to escape quietly, without running. Find a window, find a door, some way out. She wants out. She must get out. She gets nowhere; he is awake. She says she must go but he holds a twenty in one hand and a bottle in the other. He gives her the bottle and pulls her back upstairs. The water was not hot enough; the smell is still clinging there. This time she believes nothing. This time she grits her teeth.

He calls her a whore. She takes the twenty and walks, runs straight to the corner store for a bottle of wine — red, with a screw-top cap. The biggest one they sell; she makes no attempt at restraint. Rituals from a far off past no longer have any meaning; she doesn't tarry over the bouquet. She drinks straight from the bottle, raising it high in the air, her two shaking hands being careful -extra careful- to make sure it doesn't spill. Eager drops dribble down her chin. She always spills the first gulp and never stops to wipe it away.

The wine is like fresh blood in her dried up veins. Her true savior, liquid life: hot, astringent in her mouth, turning her teeth dead blue, a trail of heat and a molten ball glowing, churning, growing in her stomach, and out of it taking everything over, every synapse and corpuscle soon to be humming again in false harmony. Wine seems to quiet the echo. It banishes the voices. It makes his panting groans sound far away and dreamy, and for now it is good to have them not quite so close. For now it is good to forget, to become cloaked in a leaden haze.

She stumbles to St. Mary's; the church is double-spired and symmetrical. Perfectly balanced. "Nothing Wrong Here" is what it shouts, perfection and grace are what it touts. Its shiny tin spires are two bullet breasts aimed straight toward man's God in His Heaven. Chaste cross nipples top each spire, hard and erect and sore, withholding lifesaving spiritual sustenance and comfort.

Tears stream down her face; she does not know why. No one will ask. She stares up at Mother Mary: a clean, pristine, dustless shrine behind a pane of glass, another stone-faced visitor to her dirty prison.

Who will watch over her? Lady of Lourdes, pray for her. Oh, Lady of Lourdes, protect her. If only someone would light a candle. If only someone would say a prayer. Then she might be helped; then she might be saved. Make a donation; it is God's plan. Keep off the grass. Either she's in or she's out: Heaven or Hell. No loitering before or afterward.

Church is hard, the stones are smooth and cold. It hurts to kneel down. Prayer has become impossible. When did she become so alone? As a child she relished daily mass and thought hard about becoming a nun. Instead she became a none, inspired to silence in this beautiful but empty space, this peaceful piece of a hushed praying place. The churchyard is quiet, unusually so. Ordinarily it oozes the wounded and wailing, a way station for those on their way down. Could she be the only one left?

It is dark when she comes upon the cemetery. Her second or third or fourth jug of wine is very nearly gone. So is she. Some of the gravestones inside the locked gates are new and shiny, others so old the writing has been worn smooth. They are cracked, uprooted, twisted and in pieces beneath trees, mauled and broken by unkind Time. This is a place where life and death commingle so easily, so quietly and without argument that the line between them becomes blurred beyond distinction.

Coming here is like coming home; she enjoys spending time with the dead. Doing so makes her appear somehow more alive and less alone. She thinks about the people buried there, stacked in tomb upon tomb upon tomb, most above ground but some still buried below.

Well established families have cordoned off large plots like permanent crime scenes. Gravestones etched with names are placed in straight rows. No dates on them, though, not yet. The clean stones will wait there, confirmed reservations in a final hotel, no mints on pillows, only yellow and purple plastic flowers left to fade under an unrelenting subtropical sun.

The fence surrounding most of the cemetery is warped, stretched, and tired. A sign states that visiting hours are sunrise to six p.m.; no dogs allowed. The dead are quite strict that way. They need their rest.

Silent phantoms slip one by quiet one underneath the loose chain link, searching out vacant tombs like water seeking its own level. She creeps in along with the others, hunkering down in the dirt and crawling with the clumsy stealth of a baby. She snags her already ragged dress only once on her way under, while wondering when she will have her chance, when she will have her rest, when the voices will fade away for good.

She sits on a tombstone and sucks her bottle dry. The breeze rushes through her ears, a great flush of air swirling the voices around and around inside her head. No birds sing tonight, and the crypts are silent; happy houses of stone with only one way in and no way out. Plant life thrives all around her, bursting out of the smallest cracks in the masonry, unstoppable life sprouting green from Death's black facade, life after life on top of life on top of death.

A curious place, this old boneyard, at the same time open and closed, telling its secrets only to those who, like her, listen closely. She hears that she will be here to stay soon enough, that this life she leads is an illusion, not real.

A plane flies low overhead, the last flight of the evening. She can see the stars, an unusual sight in Key West, for most of the island is too grown up. Its magic is faded and contrived, perverted by buzzing neon, polluted with electricity. She looks up at the sky and watches it spin.

She has a queer clarity of vision as she reels and sways on her stone seat, seeing double, fully twice the twinkly stars so bright. Each glimmer stabs her haze with a bright white hope, a new hope for escape. Cemetery whispers whirl away, into diminishing darkness. It is never too late for redemption; at the end of the day all will be paid in full. She sinks to the ground, grateful to have nothing beyond these skies, this ground, this here, this now. The dark crevice in which she has hidden now sprouts the seed of desire: one more breath, one more chance, one more day-thin, but green and hungry for light. Serenity cracks the dull mask of her visage. She understands.

# THE CUBAN GODFATHER

*BARBARA BOWERS*

Michael is a doctor. A doctor and a sixth generation Sanchez family member.

He recently opened his practice in Key West, and today, he dropped by the "studio under the trees" to meet his great uncles, Mario and Perrucho. This, of course, presented Perrucho the perfect opportunity to bring out the family photos. There's papa with José Martí on the balcony of the house just around the corner. Here's the whole Sanchez clan at the the turn of the century, and that's Mario in his uncle's arms. This one's of Perrucho with some local politicos at the Cuban Club.

On another day, John brings a sepia toned photo to the garden studio. It's faded. It's obviously ancient. The ball players, the old brick building and the Key West neighborhood just can't be placed.

"It's before my time," says 85 year old Mario.

Tony, Pancho, Carlo — all the old timers — puzzle over the picture. Nope. It can't be placed. So: Figuring the past unlocks most present-day dilemmas. Perrucho brings out the family photos and newspaper clippings again.

All the comings and goings from Mario Sanchez's "studio under the trees" make it far more than an artistic stronghold for his particular brand of art. It's a perpetual flow of people ... a revolving door of personalities and opinions. It's where 19th century history is reconstructed; where politics are rehashed; and where the good 'ol days — and some of the bad — are relived in heated Spanish dialect. Most importantly, Mario's outdoor studio is a gathering place for his extended family.

Holding court like the Cuban Godfather, Mario has set up shop, and welcomed friends and family, to his brother's sideyard for the past 32 years. Cuban Conchs (Key West natives of Spanish descent) hang-out here to maintain cultural ties. His own family members congregate here to maintain blood ties. And thousands of interested visitors drop by each year to watch Mario carve and paint on wood — all wanting a little piece of his genius; all wanting to see him conjure up scenes from his youth in Key West from which he shapes his primitive images of people and places and formulates his whimsical memories of yesteryear.

But if you plant yourself amidst the bilingual bunch, listen as closely as you watch, and hang around the patio long enough, you'll learn that art is merely a byproduct of the soft-spoken Mario. La familia and legacies are his crowning achievements.

"I'm not an artist," said Mario one morning as he penciled in floor planks of the poolroom in the old Cuban Club. It was a carving commissioned by Cemetery, a poolhall buddy from years gone by.

What are you, then?

Without a second's hesitation, and without looking up from the red cedar, he said quite simply: "Married."

First and foremost, Mario is a family man. Secondarily, he is an artist ... one who was named the 1991 Florida Folk Artist of the Year and who was one of the two Key West artists profiled in the book, 19th Century American Folk Art. He is an artist who attracts 2,000 people to a Tampa Museum fund-raiser at $1,200 a head. One whose attention to detail and memory of Old Key West makes his work as important historically as it is artistically. And one who commands tens of thousands of dollars for painted woodcarvings that are commissioned by a handshake years before they're undertaken.

The pool hall scene, for instance, was requested some years back, and now as cedar chips and rough woodgrain give way to Mario's fertile imagination, its creation brings back a flood of memories and lots of Spanish chatter from the sidelines.

"Cemetery was one of the best pool shooters at the Cuban Club, and I gave him his nickname for all the fights he tried to start there," said Mario. "I told him he was a walking graveyard and the name stuck. That's him there in the carving, shooting pool left-handed."

Did you shoot pool, Mario?

"Ask Perrucho if I played pool," said the artist in his quiet, gentle manner.

This simple directive revealed the depth of his relationship with his big brother. More than a blood relative, Perrucho is the Segundo Don;

Mario's right-hand man. He is his spokesman, his biggest promoter, and Mario's foil for modesty: "Mario was champion. He even spotted Cemetery points when he was a kid," said Perrucho matter-of-factly. Out came the family photos again, and this time I was treated to stories of Alfredo deOro, who, in 1896 hustled Mario's and Perrucho's dad, then went on to become the "World Champion Shooter."

Mario smiled and listened and commented occasionally on one of the many poolhall stories circulating among the gentlemen lounging in the lawn chairs. But mostly, he rubbed his well-worn brush on the wood. He scraped away rough edges. He rubbed again. Penciled in new lines. Then rubbed some more color onto the walls of the Cuban Club. And he confided, "the hardest part is painting ... getting the colors right."

When I first met Mario and the boys, he told me his studio offered "a new floor show every day." He wasn't kidding, and he wasn't alluding to himself as the main attraction, either. He was just stating a fact and preparing me for the frequent, spontaneous moments of adult Show 'n Tell. Moments like the morning he brought out "Soap Box Rumba," a woodcarving depicting a street dance in Gato Village. It had been finished a little while back, and it was waiting to be collected by its new owners. The 1918 scene from Mario's mind froze in time a section of Key West on the outskirts of the Eduardo Gato Cigar Factory where he grew up: It was party time Cuban-style. A clown danced on an Octagon soap box. Brilliant yellows and pinks lit the sky and the cigar makers' houses. African costumes adorned some merrymakers. And even the palm trees danced and swayed to the long lost rhythms.

"Go ahead, touch it. Get a feel for it," Mario urged. Then referring to his motto painted on a wall of the garden studio, he grinned and said, "It may not be good, but it makes you smile."

Whimsical touches like the small face peeking through the bushes offered insight into a playful childhood. Apparently, a cherished childhood that has been nurtured and coddled by this aging little boy, for Mario's child-like humor is shot through and through his 450+ works of art.

In case I doubted that, John hot-footed it around the corner to get the painted carving Mario did four years ago for his son. And Oscar went home to get his Mario original of La Te Da, a rendition of the charming old Conch house Oscar's family owned before it became a well-known Key West guest inn.

Cats and roosters, kids and pregnant women — always pregnant women —bicycles, and generally, everything wonderful from childhood are worked into Mario's historic time capsules of Key West. Images in clouds and tiny signs in some of his carvings are especially subtle and layered with humor. For instance, the decorative gold cash register at the pool hall had a "No Sale" key on it. But youthful Cubans recognized it as "No Salé" - Spanish for "nothing comes out."

True to history, "No Salé" was right there in the poolhall carving he was currently scraping and painting on.

This sharp recall and penchant for historic detail is, in part, why Mario's woodcarvings have skyrocketed in value over the last 15 years. Sure, he remembers a great deal of detail himself, but Mario confessed that before his mother died, she kept him honest, and his late wife, Rosa, was also a stickler for detail. And of course, Mario admits "the old timers who come by are real nourishment."

When I arrived today, "the studio under the trees" had been converted into the cafe under the trees. Tables and tablecloths studded the patio with the usual array of lawn chairs. The old gents — always jovial — were especially atwitter on this Monday morning. And Mario's sheet-draped worktable was undraped because he wasn't working today: It was party time Cuban-style. Everybody was waiting for Cha Chi, the youngest Sanchez brother, to bring on the paella.

As Perrucho phoned his baby brother to light a fire under him, he assured me it would be the best Paella I'd ever eat. Marty juggled mangos and sighed that "this would all be over when Mario leaves for the summer season and goes back to Tampa." And Tony insisted, in spite of what the feisty ol' fellas were telling me, this was not a wedding party for him. After all, he was quite happily married to his fifth wife, thank you. This was just an impromptu feast because Riggio had caught a surplus of stone crab, and because this was Key West and a very good day for a Cuban celebration.

The Cuban Club Poolhall carving was finished by now. And like Mario's other pieces, it had taken about a month. Just this weekend he started working on a "water" scene in front of the Key West lighthouse. While the others set the table and poured soft drinks, Mario showed

me the newly drawn and freshly etched scene of an old Bahamian selling perfumed water in Cuban demi-johns. A horse drawn water-wagon
was spraying Whitehead Street to hold down the dust on a sizzling
summer afternoon. And several kids were skipping behind the wagon
to get wet; to cool off.

One of the boys was Mario. For the first time, he had carved himself
into a small piece of Key West history. Until now, the faces and figures
were always other people ... acquaintances, friends, family members. In
fact, not only had Mario never carved himself into one of his pieces, he
had never even kept one of his woodcarvings. All had been given away,
or sold upon a handshake.

Quietly, Mario explained that he "has no reason to keep them." You
see, the Cuban Godfather, and even the Segundo Don, have never
been blessed with children of their own.

# TO THE KEYS

### DEANNA O'SHAUGHNESSY

On the highway I'm heading down
out of Miami
on my way to the Keys,
the quality of the light as I drive
reminds me of a highway in Mexico City;
pale, hot, flat concrete,
under flat, hot, pale skies,
even though the light lies
about the heat,
because it's unseasonably cold.

Flying along the road to the Keys,
I glance off and see a sailboat,
like a coal burning
a black hole through
a white hot sea.
Smoky clouds like chalk drawings,
waft off the glare of the water.
A landscape blooms there, reaching
in stretches and patches,
all the way to the edge
of the sky.
A mirage of water lies
in a desert of sea,
with palm tree oasis,
floating all shimmery around the
tufty tops to ancient reefs.
Long dead coral bodies
made green by droppings
of birds flying overhead,

sprout life from the dead,
as the sea is continuously
apt to do.

Motels & eateries,
scattered among the fisheries,
pummel me with billboard signs.
And at their feet, grasses sigh
with pink feather tops
by the roadside,
next to palm trees, next to windy seas,
side-by-side with bougainvillaea
and vines climbing telephone poles
and old roadsigns for hotels
and Marine Supplies,
under hazy pewter skies with
sun glancing off the windshield
like winter rain.

House of Pancakes, Wendy's,
Herbie's & Denny's,
a sudden flurry of stoplights:
I must be in Marathon,
the King Kong of the Florida Keys,
waiting for a Fay Wray
to save it from ambiguity....
Sharks hang by their tails
outside bars where fish fables
are told over rum cocktails
at Happy Hour;
the power of the sea
brought down daily
to wrestling matches with drunks.
After the glory days of pirates
and sunken treasure,
Neptune's reputation
awaits the pleasure of

daytripper fishermen and dilettantes
that flaunt their ignorance
over pints and shots,
bought by other would-be Hemingways.
And through a thicket of poles,
where fishermen angle off bridges,
lined up in packs & groups & pairs,
the pale surface of the sea shines,
hiding its secrets in its varying depths,
where Egrets & Pelicans,
the seraphim of the islands,
ride the wind or stand
like Chinese porcelain,
knee deep in aqua seas.

My wheels slap bridges that
only fly over but
can never really cover
such mysterious territory,
merely ribbons tying together
the surprise package islands
that float ancient and serene,
seeming so insubstantial as to be
as new as last night's dream.
Tourists, sailors, fishermen, lovers,
all hover about in bars and boats,
floating their schemes, fingering
their dreams to capture the mystery
and put it in their pockets.
But the rocks wind out from under,
like the blue-green current,
never really hurried,
never completely owned,
no matter how many condos
get blown out of their limey soils.
Islands like pirates, never captured,
only dressed-up like civilians,

their wild nature not quite hidden.
We name them, stalk and claim them,
make parks and bridges,
build roads to ride them,
but inside them are the bones
of the living beings that breathe water
and will forever be more ancient
than we are.

And the car is ordered by signs
to slow to a crawl
along the section of road
we've named Big Pine,
to save the lives of the tiny
Key Deer, with tiny ears and hooves,
that tremble by the road that
cuts their home in two.
A home wearing the mismatched
shoes of two minds:
Winn Dixie and Scotty's fixed
in lines of traffic or
the solace of the Blue Hole
from which old alligators get pulled
to die alone in some unknown city.
A home, like each of these islands,
dropped from the box
of God's best jewelry,
woven in a silver alchemy
between mangrove tree
and the glittering sea;
lands birthing out of a shallow sea
with still tiny mangrove trees
cooling webby feet
in salty waters.

Jet planes assault the sky
in a wandering roar,

shuddering the road that wends
past tattoo parlors and refugee camps,
carrying refugees with skin the pallor
of fish markets,
jumping the channel markers
like the cow over the moon,
touching down hooves on
the Isle of Bones.
Home to the lost
and all that can be found,
sacred ground of the profane;
they flock to the grave
at the end of the line,
disguised in sunshine sarongs,
dancing to a sultry song
fringed in frenzied edges,
swimming over coral ledges
with no tank.
Getting tanked at noon,
clutching a bottle of booze,
or running through wreaths of
aromatic weed or opting for
the white tile illusion of serenity,
humans rung out
from the long bout with life,
lean out over the balconies of Duval
and try not to fall as they choke
on their margaritas and the smoke
rising from the beauty burning
in a cloud of exhaust.

And out, across the waters
the sun rests in clouds like
a puff of smoke,
shedding its light like gold
dripping from the lips of God.
Under the flat, hot, pale concrete,

# To The Keys

next to the painted silhouette
of plastic palm trees,
under the varying depths of
blaring human incongruities,
this is the place
where angels weep
for the beauty of aqua seas,
and bring their tears to keep
like jewels,
for the day when crowns
will be given to the Children,
and the beasts of the sea
will sing.

# Two Gentlemen in Bonds

## *KIRBY CONGDON*

"You're late," Burdick said and readjusted his rump on the low cement bulwark that separated the fishing pier at the end of White Street from the road that bordered the beaches.

"For what?" Anders asked in an automatic response as his eyes surveyed the Atlantic Ocean for the day's weather.

Burdick studied his watch. "It's almost a quarter of eight." He looked up at Anders. "You're usually here by half past."

Anders returned the gaze and with a turn of his hand indicated his own barren wrist. "I hadn't noticed." Burdick's gaze persisted, so Anders said, "I was watching TV last night. Probably slept a little longer," and to change the subject, "Look at that sunrise!"

"There was one yesterday too," Burdick replied with an aborted laugh. "What did you expect? But it's over now. The sun's been up for, I'd say, a good forty minutes. That's what I'd say." He tried being agreeable. "But I got to look that up. It's in the paper every day, you know, where the weather and all that there stuff is."

"Yes, I know." Anders settled himself on the wall.

Burdick changed the subject himself now. "Here comes that motorcycle again. Never fails. But he's late too. Probably has to go to work every morning, do you think?"

"No, he's comes back in twenty minutes with a newspaper stuck on the passenger seat."

"He's probably retired like everybody else in this place. Got nothing else to do. I give it up."

"Retirement?"

"Nah. Reading the paper." Burdick looked into the middle distance. "I used to read that paper from front to back every morning. And that was even before I went to work. Never missed reading the paper. Never missed a day's work, either."

Anders smiled a little. "And now you don't miss a day's retirement?"

Burdick ignored the question and threw his hand in a gesture toward the road. "He didn't stop." He turned toward Anders for confirmation. "There's a stop sign there."

"He stopped," Anders remarked and looked out at the pier.

"His wheels never stopped moving."

Anders brought his attention back. "He shifted gears. His rear stop light went on. What do you want him to do? If a bike stops dead, he has to put his foot down on the ground and hold that thing up. Keep it from falling over. Do you want him to take his helmet off and put on some glasses and then make the car behind him drive up his back? He stopped."

Burdick looked away, dismissing the matter. "He only slowed down."

Anders said nothing. Burdick filled in. "So he changed gears, but he didn't stop. He paused. He almost stopped but he didn't."

Anders considered the transgression for a moment. "He looks like a nice enough guy," he said.

Burdick straightened his back. "With them boots?"

"That goes with the outfit," Anders explained. "Boots are boots. Engineer boots, hip boots, motorcycle boots—"

Burdick took a breath. "Slippers. Are slippers shoes? Are shoes boots? There's boots and there's boots."

"It's part of the gear. Some dress up swell. Like him," Anders nodded toward the motorcycle as it disappeared down the road. "There's polite boots like for the king of England. There's dress boots, work boots, police boots. And there's—well—" he chuckled, "that mean black boot with chrome fittings. Those that guy had were mean black boots with chrome fittings."

"He's a fag."

"He doesn't smoke. Can't with a helmet on."

"I mean fag fag. They all come here. From New York. Guys. Together." Burdick leaned a shoulder over confidentially. "I mean together." Burdick looked at Anders' knees and moved his buttocks away by three inches. "My wife died," he said with conviction.

"Mine should have," Anders replied. Burdick's eyes bore down on Anders. Feeling accused, Anders explained. "I mean her pain. She's always in pain."

"She is?"

"Well," Anders cocked one eye. "She says she is. How would I know?"

"You don't love her?"

"What do you mean?"

"If you loved her, you'd know."

"Know what?"

"If she's in pain."

"What good would that do? Do I put my arms like this—" Anders put his arms akimbo, "and do I say, 'Are you in pain? How much is this here pain? Where's the pain-measuring stick? Huh?"

"You should know, if you love her. Do you ever tell her, like this: I love you?"

Anders winced. "After all these years?"

Burdick nodded

Anders lightened his voice artificially. "Hi, dear. Are you in pain? I love you. Do you love me? Christ! I can't say that. We've never had to make polite talk. He shrugged. "It all goes without saying."

Now Burdick winced. "It never goes without saying."

"If you have to say it, then you're just reading it. From what? Some document? So you prove it? What kind of relationship is that?"

"A relationship is a relationship."

Burdick's head lolled briefly from side to side in a private lullaby. "Relations. Relations."

"Well, we don't have those kind of relations any more."

Burdick seized the point. "You stopped loving her?"

"We didn't stop." Anders reviewed the matter. "We just paused. And the pauses—well, you know how it is; they got longer and longer." He opened his fingers and spread his arms apart. "Now it's all pause."

Burdick's head jerked in a quick no. "A long pause is a stop. It's over."

"No, it isn't."

"Well now, you just said a pause is a stop."

"Jesus! I was talking about motorcycles."

"What's the difference?"

Anders grimaced with forced patience. "One is flesh and blood. The other isn't. That's the difference. But, you know, you do get your emotions involved, as they say. I mean with a machine. I saw a man kick his bike, he was so damned mad at it. It only ran out of gas. Needed a new battery. Who knows. His best friend, and he was kicking it as though it had done him wrong!"

Burdick turned to Anders. "Friend? It's only a machine."

Anders couldn't resist. "So's a wife."

Burdick's neck stiffened. "How can you talk like that?"

"Like what?"

"Saying a wife is a machine. Like a refrigerator? An egg beater?" His voice rose almost hopefully. He wiped his neck. "An automatic air conditioner?"

"No. Like a motorcycle."

"What's so great about a motorcycle? A car, I can see. You get attached to a car."

"A car's just taking part of your living room—wherever you're going. But you never leave! You never leave home, really."

"Who wants to leave home?"

"Everybody wants to at some point. Travel. See the world. Sow their oats."

"Yeah," Burdick agreed. "Me and my wife, we went off to Pine Ridge Valley every vacation. Never missed a summer. Our trip. Thirty years we went. Everyone knew us in Pine Ridge Valley. Oh, yeah!—" he recalled. "We skipped one season, though. You know how they keep jacking up the rents. That was our protest. We stayed home. Cut the grass. Read the papers."

"But then you went back?"

"Sure did. Had to. There was no place else to go. She wasn't going anywhere besides there anyway."

"That's not leaving home—taking your wife—like I mean it. When you were young—before her—didn't you want to head out on your own, by yourself, alone?"

"Alone! Who wants to be alone?"

"You're alone now."

Burdick shrugged his shoulders as a smirk crossed his mouth. "She died."

"I know."

"Yep."

"You miss her, don't you?"

Burdick looked at Anders defensively and shook his shoulders indecisively.

"You could say."

"You must have loved her."

Burdick looked up in surprise. "No! We already had the divorce. But still, I suppose, I miss her now maybe."

"Your affection sort of comes back, then?"

"You could say that."

"Would you say your feelings, this love for her, had stopped, or had been on a pause?"

"How the hell do I know? Do you think I'm regulated like some clock? That I go fast and I go slow, and I stop and I pause or—God willing—start up?"

"No, I don't suppose so."

"You're damned right. God knows, I'm a free man. This is a free country, and I sure won't be regimented."

"Yeah. I understand where you're coming from."

"You do? Why's everything always the same to you?" Burdick demanded.

"When you agree, you know, it's like, it's like someone's come to the gates of St. Peter's and, and this someone repents his sins and all the time he's looking out the window at the view."

"St. Peter or the sinner?"

"Both."

"Yes. I guess it doesn't make much difference." Anders evaluated himself anew. "It's all the same, I suppose." He stood up.

Burdick's back straightened.

"I suppose. I suppose. This ain't no conversation."

Anders turned to look at the pier and said, "Okay. See you tomorrow."

"Well, you were here this morning, you were here yesterday and the day before, so I suppose you'll be here tomorrow."

"Probably," Anders replied helplessly. Walking away, he looked back at Burdick. Burdick chanted after him: "Probably. Probably. The whole world's one big 'Probably.'"

Burdick watched Anders' departure, surveyed the sky, and now he was the one who took in the pier. His head bobbed up and down thoughtfully like that of a man who was reflecting on the certainty of some things and, as well, on the uncertainty of others. He smiled to himself; not *everyone's* a thinker.

# I, OLIVIA

## *MARGIT BISZTRAY*

My name is Olivia Cameron-Diaz and I have been dead half a century. I lie in a plot in the Key West cemetery, holding a pair of small shoes and a book.

The shoes were my mother's first ones, sewn by her father, a sailor named Hector. If you could examine them, you would see that sixteen delicate stitches form every inch of the seams, which is remarkable considering my grandfather's hands were so large that he was famous the length of the Florida Keys for being able to enclose a conch shell in one.

"Hector could open coconuts like this —— PA-CRACK!"

"He unlocked the jaws of a baby nurse shark from Winky Mingo's left shin. He spread the jaws like a paper fan!"

I heard the stories my whole life. I heard them so many times, of course I believed them. I never saw his hands since grandfather drowned before I was born.

Yes, he drowned. The man who raced out to sea during storms to save the cargo of sinking ships, Hector the Wrecker, at one time the third richest man in Key West, couldn't swim a lick. He said, "I sail. I eat fish. But swim? Never!" And when his vessel finally capsized during a storm they called Faith, grandfather sank without protest. That's what a witness said: "Hector the Wrecker sank without protest."

Grandmother liked the idea that he didn't protest. She said it meant he drowned peacefully or, if not, that he was dead before the ship even sank. In either case, she knew he died without suffering. She had the words "Died in his sleep" carved on his headstone, which is misleading because it suggests things like a bed and the dark of night, when in fact he died wet, wearing boots, shortly after lunchtime. Grandmother said that it didn't matter with what precision the words on a gravestone described someone's death, their philosophy, or whether they went to church. The words had nothing to do with the dead, she said, but were inscribed for the living and for the unborn. "Read the stones," she said.

69

"This man, a husband. This one a father and a grandfather. You see? That is what matters, Olivia."

Grandmother, who was a midwife, understood life and death, and how we cannot hold either, no more than we can hold light. When she and I passed through the cemetery, we stopped in a certain corner where stones no larger than footprints lay. Walter, born on October 15, died on October 16. Eunice, a five-year old. Beloved Daisy and Ricky, twins taken by a fire. Betsy who drowned at age seven. Infant deaths. Miscarriages. A murdered son. I learned that my life and story were already special. I had been born and survived.

My mother, unlike her father, swam like a fish. As a girl, she beat the boys in both front and back stroke, and could dive deeper and stay under longer than children twice her age. At thirteen, she went with her uncle Amos, who was my grandfather's brother and swam no better than he, to Sand Key lighthouse to see his friend Ralph, the keeper there. On the return trip she jumped from the boat, saying she'd see Amos back at home. Amos said he never rowed as hard as he rowed that day. He never cursed as hard either.

After that, both Amos and Hector Cameron vowed never to take Louisa or anyone like her out in their rowboats. But when the brothers visited Ralph, harvested conch by Big Mullet key, or caught mangrove snapper in the Gulf of Mexico, Louisa swam near their boats. At least it looked like Louisa. What other girl or woman swam as she did? Hector believed it was she and did his best to keep her inside, on land. He scolded her, but she just bowed her wet, tangled head and ignored his words. "Dry off," he ordered. Her wetness bothered him. "Stop swimming all the time." It bothered him that she could do something he could not. She was his daughter, his little girl. She shouldn't be so mysterious. "My daughter's not of this world," he complained to the other men.

Locally, people believed a mermaid haunted the Camerons. When Hector drowned, they said the mermaid had tipped his boat, claiming him finally. "She'll come for Amos next," they said. Whether he feared the fulfillment of such prophesies, or whether his distrust of water and all that could swim finally surmounted his bravery, Amos quit wrecking and sold his boat for a song and moved as far from the sea as possible, to somewhere called Iowa.

Grandfather said that my mother's shoes made her behave like a mermaid. Because you see, when she started walking, there was no leather available, at least not the soft, easy to sew kind of leather, so Hector made the shoes out of fish skins. "From the beginning, her feet belonged to the sea," Hector moaned. "It is my fault. My fault," he said, burying his face in his giant hands.

When she was fifteen, a boat of Norwegian sailors en route to Haiti stopped in Key West. When the ship sailed, Louisa went away with it. "The fish has disappeared," Hector said. "We will not see her again."

When she returned, she carried me in her belly. Hector took one look and vanished into the bars. "My daughter carries a fish-child," he said, ordering rum drinks for everyone. "This child will be uglier than a jewfish, with skin as cold as raw shrimp. My life is over as of this day."

Some say he finished his drink and crushed the glass in one hand. Some took his words as a premonition of his own death. The mermaid (said others) made his suspicions reality, but with an unforeseen twist. According to grandmother, the only real problem was Hector's hatred of foreigners. "If only he could have seen you," she used to tell me. "You look like him, but with such strange, light blue eyes."

My mother told me my foreign father came from a land of white trees.

My mother's stories were beautiful. She told me how the Keys came into being, a story which went like this: A long time ago the first mother lived at the top of the earth, closest to the sun, where she had a perfect view. The trees grew flowers which bloomed into fruit, which fed the birds and turned them yellow and green and red. Butterflies swooped through the air, which smelled of ginger and frangipani. The sea fell and curved endlessly around the edge of this paradise, and sometimes boats chanced upon the mother's island, bringing her gifts of seashells and fish.

But then the boats began staying. Instead of waves, their wooden sides slapped the shoreline. Their masts jabbed at the sky as if to pierce it with holes. The sailors ate all the fruit so that the birds became hungry. One day the great mother announced she'd had enough of these sailors. "Too many men have come to this garden," she said, "I will go make my home elsewhere." And so she left, taking the birds and the butterflies with her, and went to the island now called North America.

But the men chased her, following her through the forests, mountains, and deserts, until she stood at the tip of a long hot peninsula, staring at the sea. She knew that to thwart these adventurers would require all her powers. She sang to the sea and called up dolphins and whales, who carried gigantic rocks from the ocean's bottom, and strung these rocks in a broken necklace. From North America's edge, she built a trail over a hundred miles long, and then she skipped to the end of it, where one cold and one temperate sea held hands. Although many ships tried to pursue her, most met their end on the shallow rocks. The gold and treasures from these ships washed up on shore at the mother's feet, which she didn't mind a bit. Sailors who did reach the final rock in the hundred mile chain were those with interesting stories and excessive bravery, sorts that she preferred, whom she permitted to stay.

My mother told me Key West belongs to the kind of women who hide from most men, and men attracted to that kind of women.

My mother's stories explained almost everything, so as a child I had no unanswered questions. Now as an adult —- and as a dead one, at that —- I have two questions and not an answer to either one. The first concerns my dead neighbor, Emma. Unlike the rest of us, whose living relatives flaunt our identities for all the dead to appreciate, Emma is left alone. On Memorial Day, Christmas, Easter, and Veteran's Day, when all the rest of us wear silly wreaths and pots of seasonal flowers, Emma lies undecorated. The only time I heard Emma recognized was when a couple, the woman pregnant, passed by her grave and the man exclaimed, "Emma! If it's a girl why not Emma?" To which the woman replied, "Emma's a good name indeed."

Since she was buried when I arrived here, I have no idea how Emma came to the cemetery. I don't believe she was lonely. I do believe she was loved. She feels too warm in the space beside me to have been lonely or unloved. I think she died out of place, brought on a ship that met its fate on the water. Then Emma washed up on shore, wearing a pendant inscribed with her name perhaps? Or else she came here in search of someone, but died before they were introduced. The only thing anyone knew was that she called herself Emma. This was a long time ago, when people didn't ask questions. Now she's a mystery and she is restless. I hear her scratching, a dry, husky, restless sound. She shifts and flops, as if she still needs to do something. I hope to learn more, perhaps through a visitor. This may take years, but that doesn't worry me. These days I have time to wait.

The other question is, who was Ethan? I barely knew the man since at the time when my mother married him I was not speaking to anyone. I lived with her then, and one day she said, "I'm going to live with the gardener. We're getting married" and I thought, "To that old man? Why?" but didn't ask her, being too occupied with my own grief.

He only lived five years more, and I believed Ethan had always been old. He had been put on this earth so that my mother might have a husband, if just in the nick of time. Before he died he built a wall of beach glass and seashells around the house they shared, and I believe it still stands. From a short distance, the glass designs spell "Louisa," but just from one vantage point, if one knows where to look.

I never knew until mama died that Ethan's body lay in the Jewish part of the cemetery, where mama joined him. Had mama known he was Jewish? Had she converted? Where did Ethan come from with such a strange accent? Who knew? Did mama know? I ask her now, through the graveyard. She shrugs and tells me she's tired and has no more stories. "Ethan loved me," she murmurs. "Isn't that enough? Stop asking questions, Olivia."

I feel her turn towards his body. I feel her hands reach for the sides of her coffin as if she might find him there. I hear her enter the sleep that lasts many years. I try to rest as she does, but find it difficult with all my questions and with all of the voices here.

"Why are there so many voices, mama? So many dead people?"

"Most people are dead, Olivia."

The gravel shakes with conversations like mine and mama's. The talk is endless, sometimes incoherent, but always truthful. The dead don't lie because we know lies are useless now. Of course we lied in our lifetimes, but those lies became truths as they became what took place. What I mean is that we tell no new lies. We don't rewrite history. So when dead Catherine says to dead Caroline, "Your son is handsome, just like his father," dead Caroline responds, "Yes, he is," knowing, though not including, that her son's father was not her husband, but Catherine's. This detail no longer matters. The stories happen, and lies and all become history.

What matters now is how the stories continue on. The weight above me of all my children. My children's children becoming grownups. The

---

way my stories and my identities became my family's. Mother, Grandmother, Wife — I am Olivia, inscribed for the living.

People pass through the graveyard riding their bicycles, jogging, wearing the sandals sewn in the factory here, which make a pleasant click-flop! sound. Sometimes, they picnic, bringing the smells of con-leche coffee and crisp Cuban toast.

Some come here to cry, to be alone, to read books.

The poet comes around sunset, her clothing jingling and jangling. Her perfume stirs my dead nostrils, stinging them like a sneeze. Her voice is brash, slightly hysterical, shouting of things I never even dared whisper. We dead pretend we aren't listening. "I am your pussy-whore, witch, wicked vestibule." The ground goes stiff with our listening. "Your cock exquisite crows Dubonnet through my vast velvet slit dripping on sleeping vulva, unzipped nagging fruit." The dusty dead begin shuddering.

Later at night, the lovers steal through the graveyard fence. They trip around the low stones, huddle between the stacked boxes. They read our names aloud. Laugh at them. Pull corks from bottles and share grapes between their mouths. They kiss. Drink more wine. Kiss more ardently. Below, the dead heave collective sighs, thinking their private thoughts. Margaret, the graveyard prude begins twittering, "It's such an outrage! An outrage! Somebody stop them, tell them to leave. Someone frighten them! Tsk-tsk!"

More sounds of kissing, more wet sounds. The sound of buttons freed from their buttonholes. Through the commotion, I hear Raphael whispering my name. "Olivia? Remember? Remember us?"

To which I answer, "Of course I do. Your house on Donkey Milk Lane. The way the shadows of palm fronds patterned the ceiling there. Dancing the Charleston on your red, Parisian rug. The rug against my bare back and your hips on top of mine .... oh stop it, Raphie! Oh stop, I'm getting upset again!" Raphael pleads apologies. I call out, "Josephine! Josephine, do you hear this?"

And she says, "Are you still bringing that up? My god!"

And my best friend, Angela, screams, "Of course she is, tart! You stole her man from her! You stole Raphael."

Voices defend Josephine.

Her babies bawl from the children's graveyard.

Margaret huffs and puffs, "Outrage!"

Somewhere towards Frances Street, a male voice sings opera. I'm
sure it's William, the tenor. He hates graveyard quarrels.

We are most vocal during a full moon. The moon's liquid light flows
through the graveyard, seizes our bones and stirs our now bloodless
bodies. We feel, as amputees feel their missing limbs, what it is like to
contain the tides, and we lie restlessly while unresolved issues toss on
the waves no longer crashing inside of us. I do admit that I think of
Raphael when the full moon or other elements arouse my passions and
drown sensibility. Even before Raphie and I begin reminiscing, I hear
my good husband, Manuel, express understanding. He says, "I know
you, Olivia. I knew you seventy years ago. I love you all the time, dar-
ling."

His voice sounds like cello notes.

He was so small and so shy, and yet such a man. He watched me
pace in my mother's garden, curing my broken heart. He did not balk
when I ripped at hibiscus throats, tore at my clothing, sucked Spanish
limes dry. When I hurled a flowerpot at my house, he bought me another one. When I kicked my mailbox to smithereens, he nailed it together. When I did not venture out of the garden to buy myself food, he left
me baskets of bread, bananas, smoked cobia. But best of all, Manuel
brought me a lovely, blue pen.

I started writing as if I'd been given new air to breathe. I wrote a
whole book of stories called *I, Olivia* and found the selves I had lost, all
of them stronger than my grieving, angry one. I found the daughter of
a blue-eyed foreigner who sailed from a land of white trees and took a
mermaid to Haiti. I found the granddaughter of a drowned treasure
hunter and a midwife. I found my place on the island so few are privi-
leged to reach, where nectar hides in the folds of flowers and treasures
wash up on shore. In *I, Olivia*, my hurt and heartbreak ran like two
threads in an intricate fabric, no more significant than the hurts and
heartbreaks of those before me.

When I had finished, I called out to Manuel and asked him to come
eat a banana sandwich with me. He crept from the garden thicket
where he had hidden, and walked in my front door.

I never wrote again. I left the stories behind and I left five children.
It is not a bad pair of accomplishments, and I lie among the dead as
proud, if not a little bit prouder, of what I made of my life. Manuel

worked as a sponger and he provided for his family. We lived on conch, jewfish, turtle, shrimp, plantains—-the local fare — and we owned a little house on a quiet street. Our children —- Frances, Fernando, Amelia, Hector, Marie-Louisa—-know where they came from and how the Keys came to be. Anything else, they'll have to learn for themselves. I hear them now, so contemporary with their talk of cruising ships, new cars, cholesterol, and movies, which they refer to as "videos." Their children's children dance at their feet, talking all at once. Angela, my best friend, calls me the "banyan tree": the one with many roots.

I always knew that Emma heard my large family, and I felt guilty. Then, my Frances's granddaughter, Rose, announced she would bring flowers to Emma's grave "because she has none." She also promised to name her next dolly Emma, which she did because I heard her sing "Emma, here is another Emma, the same as you but not like you, because you're not dead," and then she kissed the doll, and Emma scratched beside me and twitched restlessly. Then Rose cried, "Look, daddy, look! A butterfly with one wing! How can it fly with one wing? Where is the other wing, daddy?"

The damaged butterflies fly low among the stones. The grass is littered with empty bottles and fallen vases. Plastic and silk flowers pale in the sun. Rain rubs the names from stones, which look like stubs of chalk. Not much remains of anything you might recognize.

"Most people are dead, Olivia."

"I know, mama. Isn't it interesting?"

# For Zeb, Age Two
or
## I'm Sorry, I Just Can't Have This Conversation Right Now

*DANNE HUGHES*

I'm sorry, I just can't have this conversation right now
about my life/your lovers/what's next/who's winning/
plugged in/turned on/tuned in/on line/
marketed/sold
my hair is standing on end
you see

you don't see
and neither do I
see
anything that matters much
right now

except spending some time
with this two year old boy
who speaks in tongues-fantastic
up to date ongoing conversations
using his entire body...and lots of laughter
as we dig toes in the sand
bury the picnic macaroni and
call for the next wave
to flood our hole & make a pool

grunts and snorts work very well
in this repartee-and eyes
we just bust out laughing
when we catch each other's roguish eyes
mine somewhat veiled by 50 years of living
his wide-open clear incorrigible delighted unrepentant

# For Zeb, Age Two

shrewd unanalytic
it's the current wave has him in stitches now
I float, he mimics in his rubber tube
capsizing backwards in hilarity

time to leave now
NO!
he knows what he wants and
he's not yet socialized enough for what's to come:
he's perfect like the weather, capricious
switching from fair to foul with no preamble or excuse
howling if the game goes on too long
because some fool adult got involved
and started thinking

his games go on the exact length of time
he's interested in them-no more no less-
from fascination into laughter
through to tears and then to sleep
worn out with pleasure...and some pain

I'm sorry, I just can't have this conversation
with you
right now
because, you see,
I can only speak Zebedese
not very well, mind you,
but enough to share the odd few hours
delighting in a wild mind
where desire is action &
frustration torture

no compromise is leaching- yet
the light from his fair face
and my own face forgets its history
empties almost gay; and when we're

## Danne Hughes

stopped by a parade of power boats
crawling trailered to the sea
I see the venomous colors, the hard seductive lines
more gently through his comic strip eyes
while from the thicket of a language
still not yet quite ours
his words untangle: I WANT BOAT

&

you shall have one, little mariner,
if desire remains your rocket
shoots you where your heart must go

your bright lust is a tonic
for my too guilty age

# THE PRINCESS AND
# THE PIRATES

## *DEANNA O'SHAUGHNESSY*

A story? You say you want me to tell you a story about this town. This pirate town is full of stories. There are a million of them on this little white rock floating out here at the end of the known world. A pirate town this is; it always has been, ever since Bluebeard dragged his salt-soaked swag through the mangroves, and it always will be.

After Bluebeard there were the wreckers; pirates in white cotton, keeping a weather eye peeled for treasure going down in the unlighted waters off the reef. Even the preacher in his pulpit kept his rivals pinned to their pews so he could get the jump on a sinking cargo, declaring to his parishioners, as he reached the church doors, "Wreck ashore! Now we will all run the race and see who receiveth the prize. Run that ye may obtain!"

The cigarmakers came next, but they are gone now. And what a shame, too, for the cigarmakers from Cuba were the one touch of class this town ever really had. Cubans with their clean white shirts and pastel houses. Their factories were made elegant with the soft sibilant sound of Spanish filtering through the smokey slatted sunlight as the readers read poetry and stories to ease the rollers' long hours of monotonous work. Truly civilized, though even they were fomenting revolution in their Social Clubs.

And then, of course, once the government-installed lighthouses put the salvagers out of business, there were the smugglers. Booze, Chinamen, guns. The smugglers are still here, bringing in loads of cocaine and weed from the Southern Americas, or refugees from Cuba, often dropping unwanted bodies in the shallow waters of the thin sea where they will soon enough become fish-food caught in the webs of twisting mangrove root.

Flagler, with his railroads and hotels, was the silk-lined city pirate that introduced a whole new breed of the Brotherhood to the Keys.

# The Princess and The Pirates

These have encroached like kudzu weeds, like shoots from a root too insidious to dig out, spoiling for plunder with fists full of condo contracts, consuming land where once there was a bit of quiet limestone or salty marsh. They replant paradise with Conch trains and sunset sails hoping to seduce any *turista* delusional enough to think that the real Key West still exists.

This town teeters at the edge of the world. The end of the line; it all falls away and there is nothing more beyond this place but dragons and Cuba. They all tumble down here eventually, the homeless, the lost, the wanna-bes who couldn't or didn't or shouldn't have. And here and there, just to keep you on your toes, a few who did, really Did, or are even still Doing. You never know who you're talking to down here; the scruffy guy with three days growth and the greasy baseball cap slouching along just ahead of you in line for *con leche* at the Cuban place on White St. could be another Hemingway. Pulitzers reside with as little pomp and circumstance under the palm fronds in the gardens of Old Town as do the scorpions and the soothsayers and the cats.

But not all incognitos are *literati*. Some are just garden-variety criminals; con men, thieves, parole jumpers, even murderers and extortionists. Even your lover could be undercover or in the witness protection program. Down here you never know. It's hard to tell the pirates from the princes; they all dress alike. You've got to ride a lot on gut instinct and even the most savvy of us get taken too often to blush anymore. After all, we do live in a pirate town.

There are some pirates who don't dress up or down. The streetdogs. The drugged-out, lucked-out, broken down rag-tags who have fallen down to the bottom of the world. It's usually warm enough here for most of the street dogs, two as well as four-legged, to live an insouciant life in the salt marshes or sleeping under the palms of Higgs Beach. Last winter's heavy rains and winds were a chilling reminder, though, that we do live in "louver-land," and there is no getting in out of the storm when you live on a skim of rock only 2 miles by 5 in the middle of a lot of water. Even the well-built houses, which are few and far between, and cost a king's ransom, are not immune to the insidious wind and damp slithering in under doors and curling the paint on windowsills or walls.

One had to pause and wonder how the tired old vets out in Hamaca Park were staying dry, hunkered down into sodden bedrolls with only a fifth of Old Glory to keep them warm.

But, still, most of the time it's warm here; a good place to land with no money and no prospects . . . as long as you don't expect a roof over your head. The landlords on this jammed little rock are the most proficient pirates of all. Robber barons, with few exceptions. A home is not a home in the *sanctum sanctorum* of supply and demand; it is strictly business.

During the winter is when landlords make their big bucks and the average Joe has to have a roommate and 2 or 3 jobs just to crack the monthly nut. The cool months, not the steamy ones, are the money-makers for everyone. No one makes much money when the cicadas buzz as loud as electricity in the wires and the only time dogs cross the street is to find a thin line of shade to relieve the glaring heat. The days are heavy and sleepy then. And they used to be quiet. Empty. No money, but no "crazy" either. Lately, though, some of those point eight million visitors who wend their way here every year to get out of the cold somewhere else seem to be spilling over into the summer time.

But, generally in the summer, when the city starts tearing up roads and pouring asphalt, promising to be finished by season, (which they never are), the snowbird population heads out for their nests elsewhere: New York, New Jersey, New Hampshire, Boston or the Cape. And when the water you swim in is a bit warmer than your bathwater, and the air has edges if you turn too quickly, even the tattered old beach crows begin to ride back out onto the highways from which they came. They follow the one and only long and skinny road out of here, heading north to anywhere where the afternoon showers come in cooler flavors and the thunderheads aren't bigger than the little strip of land or boat you've got your toes curled around.

So, how am I supposed to choose just one story out of all these surrounding me, floating in and out with the tides, riding the wind like the blowing seeds that made this little hunk of limestone key vegetative?

So many of the stories on paradise seem to be about love, and especially love gone wrong, or at least hard. And, though famous people abound here, most of the stories do not seem to be about them. Most of the stories are small, human stories, almost ordinary stories of tattered love and sweaty miseries rubbing up against each other in the heat. Stories all tumbled down together, to the end of the world, rough and smooth, spirited here by this Rock that's been singing the same siren song since the Indians came to fight their ancient wars and leave their old bones behind.

Though there are many, I won't tell you one of the hurtful stories; there are so many of those here in paradise that, when we hear another we just look at each other and say, "Well, we do live in Key West, don't we?"

No, I'll tell you a story that is just as sweet as jasmine on black velvet air, or bottle-green seas, luminous in the dark, whispering on the sands of South Beach; a story with a heart that burns with the color of the blossoms on the Poincianas in May. I will tell you a story without felons or alcoholics or murderers. No drunken sailors. A story without screams in the dark, ambulance or police sirens two blocks away, the eviction notice or the cleared-out bank account or the faithless employer. I'll tell you a story that doesn't even remember the town fathers paving the parking lots or building another set of inferior condos in too small a space. Just give me a minute. I know I can think of one. . .

> There was a Young Woman, a golden one, who had come from another land where she had lived with her Mother and her Sister, who were both golden, too. She had come from a land where the Sun was a star and the waters were midnight blue, and she came from afar to live on a White Island that floated quietly in the shadow of the Sun, far away in aqua seas.
>
> And this Young Woman moved like a lily and her smile was like a clear brook and she had eyes as quiet as the evening sky. The Young Woman had words in her fingertips and they flowed like cool white wine onto the fine papers she fashioned with flowers and grasses. And all of her Friends, and she had many who loved her, loved her very much.
>
> And it came to pass that this wonderful Young Woman

began to sail on a great sailing vessel out on the aqua seas, out into the stiff breezes of the Gulf waters. She scanned the warm and salty seas with a mother's eyes, warning all strangers who came to this beautiful island that was now her home, warning the strangers not to touch the creatures of the seas. In her gentle voice, she would tell the strangers about the living heart of the coral and she would warn the strangers in words made strong with love, that touching the creatures would surely kill them.

And on this great sailing vessel there were many beautiful people who scanned the seas and protected the reef with the Young Woman. But one, One, a Young Man, loved her. He was as fair as she, and his voice wove with hers, though she did not hear it at first, as she scanned the seas. But, he loved her, and he spoke to her quietly and he loved her constantly, and eventually she heard his voice rise through the waters. And when they turned their eyes to each other, they were the same color, and their laughter tumbled like lovers, and they took each other's hands, and they came to make a home together. They made a home that hovered high in the trees, fragrant with breezes, and it was white and filled with light and tapestries of fabric and flowers; bougainvillaeas gleamed like rose wine, reflected in the floors they polished bright each night with the soft steps of their dancing.

And the Young Woman pressed her fingers to her mouth and put her words on grassy papers and the Young Man looked to see and turned his eyes to touch the silver-coated films and put his visions on silver-coated papers, and their words and their visions made all their Friends, and they had many that loved them, love them very much.

And one day, one amazing summer day, the amazed Young Woman and the amazed Young Man knew that the two of them would be three. And they told their Friends, who loved them very much, to prepare for a New Year when there would be one more to love. And the Young Woman grew a child. And she grew the child as she would scan the sea with a mother's eyes. She grew the child with the words in her fingertips as she pressed them to her belly. She grew her child in her Nordic body under Tropic skies, in warm blue and salty waters. Her child grew like the bougainvillea or jasmine, as sweet as honey on the night air, and she gave him the colors and the fragrance of the sweetness. She played the music of the days for him. She laid her Young Man's head to her belly so that he could see his visions for their child. He laid his hands on her belly so their child could hear their laughter tumble like lovers and the child would know what a wondrous world awaited him, awaited with great expectations, to love him. The Young Woman's golden Mother and golden Sister came from the land of the midnight waters to await him. And all the Friends of the Young Woman and the Young Man, who loved them, watched each day, and they waited for him with amazement and they loved him very much.

But, when the day came for the child to arrive, he said it was such a lovely world inside the Young Woman's belly, he thought he might stay for just a little while longer. And the Young Woman and the Young Man held their breath and held their hands and bided the time. They would tell their child, "Come out! Come out and play with us!" They would tell their child of how they would hold him in their arms and rock him in the shadows of the palm fronds. They would hum to him all the songs of white sails on aqua seas. Each day they asked him to come make the two of them three. How they longed to look into his eyes and see that they were as blue as the sky that kissed them "Good Morning!" that very morning.

And finally, finally, after she had waited patiently for many impatient days, the Young Woman knew the baby was ready to leave her seas and see the world . . . but not very. But, the Young Woman, who moved like a lily and protected the seas like a mother, was very brave. And the Young Woman turned her blue eyes in to watch her child, and then she closed them and began.

She wrestled mightily for what seemed like days, wrestled for what could have been a lifetime. The Young Man touched *her glistening lips and kissed her dripping brow. Her golden Sister and her golden Mother rubbed her aching back and shoulders and whispered Strong Love while the Young Woman crossed many dangerous waters. The Young Woman looked with a mother's weary eyes across the great long hours and finally whispered to her child, "It is time. It is time now, and I will show you how we wrestle with Life and how we win."*

*And then he was here! Blue. A golden child, like his golden mother, the Young Woman, as beautiful as a brook, as clear as the sky, and as tired as the sea after a storm. And the Young Man and the Young Woman and her golden Mother and her golden Sister all gathered the Baby Boy, golden and shining, eyes as blue as the sky that kissed him welcome that morning, and they held him up to the palm trees, who bowed their joy, and they held him up to the scudding white clouds, who wept their delight into the turquoise seas.*

*And soon, all the Friends of the Young Woman and the Young Man, who loved them very much, came, one by one to see the golden boy named Blue. And the boy's blue eyes gathered them in, and as they touched his tiny toes, the poets poured their words over his head like Holy Waters. As he gathered them in, their visions swayed like shadow and light through their words and into his tiny ears and over his tiny lips. And the Young Woman watched and she heard and turned to words each of his breaths. And the Young Man listened and he saw and made images of his Golden Two, that made Love Herself sigh and clap Her hands. And the Young Woman and the Young Man and their bright boy, Blue, and all their friends who loved them, loved each other very much on the White Island, floating quietly in the shadow of the Sun, far away in aqua seas.*

And so, I've told you a story. And it is only one story out of the many many.

It is a small story, a human story, a love story; the story I want you to remember about paradise: a little story hiding in the grotto gardens with the Pulitzers and the pirates and the cats. There are so many stories of love taking place every day on this little white rock; stories whispering next to phosphorescent seas, taking their own sweet time under fierce stars, or sleeping quietly in out of the sun. There are so many here in paradise, that when we hear another, we just look at each other and say, "Well, we do live in Key West, don't we?"

# A Better Time, A Better Place

## WILLIAM WILLIAMSON

It's strange how a particular smell, even one of an unknown origin that you can't pinpoint, can release an avalanche of old memories and feelings from a certain time frame from your past.

A scent that smolders into your consciousness, bringing on a déjà vu trance, a remembrance of a childhood, of a day, of some buried moment that inexplicably rises from the depths in a sensory swell of indulgence that floods over reality, beaming you transfixedly back to when the event took place. The pungent aroma of guava lying in squalid ferment in the sand, overripe, crawled over by troops of ants, pecked by small birds, sends me back to that sweltering summer papa passed away from a massive heart attack protecting what he loved.

I was sixteen that summer and papa, stubborn, cantankerous, but still gentle in his own grizzled way, was sixty-six. He was ancient compared to my friends' parents; they mistook him for my grandfather, which embarrassed me. But when I think back, he was the best father a boy could have. I only wished I realized that then. When you're growing up time is on your side and you can be pretty selfish with your thoughts and actions. Papa taught me how to fish and swim, work hard for a living, and be a man, while enjoying the outdoors and respecting it enough to leave it untouched so my children could enjoy it one day.

Growing up on Matecumbe Key, a mangrove-surrounded island ninety miles from the mainland shaped papa's appreciation and understanding of the beauty and delicateness of nature that he later taught me. Our existence depended on the tropical water that surrounded us. We fished and trapped for crawfish and stonecrab, selling to fish houses and a few restaurants.

At the time I remember thinking how distasteful papa's daily attire was, his stained khaki trousers, laceless deck shoes splattered with paint with worn toe holes, a wrinkled ball cap creased down the bill

89

smelling of sweat and ringed with salt. How meager our lives seemed, how absurd it seemed to watch my parents late in the afternoon marvel at the sunset that was a ritual when they had seen it everyday of their lives, and it bored me as much as holding hands, saying grace before dinner did.

I compared my life and family to the families flocking down from the north, building new homes, establishing new businesses that made real money, their sons working after school instead of doing chores, driving new speedboats and cars to school. I was born here, but I was still riding the school bus and it seemed so unfair.

Papa stormed from the storage shed, a long string of profanity punctuating the early morning air that was already hot and humid without his steaming voice. I stood with a mouth full of avocado, looking out the open window at papa turning furiously in half circles with a baseball bat sized piece of lignum vitae in his hands. I knew the rats had gotten into our supplies again. Not the field rats that were brown and grayish, the color of marsh rabbits and stupid and easy to trap, but lighter colored, almost silver, and striped; I called them tiger rats. Papa called them other things, and I knew only the tiger rat would make him that angry. They were much smarter than the common field rat, avoiding the traps papa sat out, but carefully stealing the bait anyway. They seemed to have an appetite for anything, including slabs of smoked fish we hung from the rafters with rope, gnawing through the line to get at the meat from the floor. Papa had only managed to kill two of them over the years. One he shot, the other drank poison he set out. They seemed to learn from the other's mistakes, papa said, so he took the poisoned rat and hung it outside on our buoy line between two sapodilla trees as a warning. But they still came around taking what they wanted while skillfully avoiding the spring-loaded traps that the field rats would carelessly step into. In the morning, if there was evidence of chewing and tampering and the bait stolen from the wooden traps then papa would go into a tirade cursing the elusive tiger rat. Myself, I had only seen about a half dozen tiger rats on the island and two of them were dead, so to me they didn't seem like the nocturnal culprits papa made them out to be.

One morning two men in armpit-stained business suits, sweating profusely and looking as out of place as fish on land, came to our house.

They said they were representing the man who had bought the Johnsons' place on the west side of the island and had a proposition to offer papa. We had no idea the Johnsons had sold out, but we knew both of them had been sick and were staying on the mainland with family. They stated they were instructed to offer cash amounts to papa and the other three families left on the island for their property. When their intentions were made clear, papa exploded, ordering them off his land, threatening to shoot them and feed them to the sharks before they even told us how much money they were offering. They snatched up their papers and folders, fleeing down the porch steps and out of the yard like chickens scattering. Before they took to the worn trail that ran through a hardwood hammock down the middle of the island to the other side, one of them turned and shouted what they would pay. Papa answered by raising his old carbine towards them till their footsteps and voices faded into the trees. It was an incredible sum they offered; Papa was a fool not to consider it, I thought.

All day papa kept his rifle close by as he repaired broken crawfish traps, nailing new 1 x 2 strips in place, and cursed the men, the Johnsons, tourists, developers, money, and tiger rats.

I asked mama about the incredible sum of money the men were offering. She looked at me dumfounded and said, what would we do with all that money? I tried to reason with her, saying we could buy a house closer to town, closer to church where she could go more often like she said in the past. She said she didn't need a lot of money to go to church more often, she just has to pick herself up and go. "Your father could never leave this island," she told me. "Why, it's his life, his blood, he would die of a broken heart within a year if you took that away from him."

The next day a light southerly breeze rustled the treetops and the scent of guava lay heavy in the air. I was gathering the cast net and five gallon buckets to throw for baitfish when the stillness of morning was ruptured by the menacing sound of machinery on the other side of the island. I looked at papa's face, the crisp wrinkles, the white stubble around his mouth, and in his eyes I saw something I never saw before, hurt and pain that didn't need tears to be felt. He turned away, at once, walking into the shed. I kind of hoped he would come out yelling about the tiger rats' latest forage but he didn't. When he did come out, he walked slowly, dejectedly by me going inside the house. The screen door slammed and papa stomped from the porch with his carbine, mama behind him pleading with him, asking what he was doing. "Don't worry what I'm doing, worry what they're doing," was all he said as he headed down the trail towards the destructive grinds on the other side of the island. I ran after him.

Under the shaded canopy of gumbo limbo and pigeon plum trees, papa hastily walked the trail. The birds that were usually chattering and singing in the trees were silent or gone, frightened away by the man-made noise that was getting closer and louder. Already our island, our home, seemed under siege by strangers.

As we came out into the sunlight, four men stood under an ancient tamarind tree, the biggest one on the island, looking up at its giant spread and feathery foliage. A man was down on one knee, pull-starting a chainsaw. Another was operating a small bulldozer in the distance, piling vegetation in heaps. Papa raised his rifle and fired a shot that whined over their heads. They turned to look at us while the one man stood up, the chainsaw buzzing to life in his hands. Papa fired another round; the chainsaw fell to the ground as all four retreated, running to safety behind the bulldozer, the one man clutching his side. Papa turned the chainsaw off, emptied the gasoline on the ground, then sat down leaning against the furrowed bark of the tamarind tree.

An hour passed when Sheriff Pinder walked up accompanied by one of the men that had come to our house the day before. Papa stood up, his rifle hanging limply in one hand pointed at the ground. The sheriff nodded curtly at me and asked papa what he was doing shooting at innocent men. Papa was silent, staring at the stranger mopping his brow with a handkerchief. Sheriff Pinder told us the Lowes, the Roberts, and the Johnsons' had sold out to Mr. Rodrieguez, leaving papa's place and the Arnolds, who only came down in the winter, remaining on the island. Mr. Rodrieguez was going to develop the island into a first class resort, and there wasn't much we could do about it except put up with the noisy construction, and that would commence as soon as all the permits were in order with the Department of Natural Resources. Papa asked about the birds that migrated to the island in the winter, fewer returned every year, the development would keep them completely away. "That's all being looked into," the sheriff said.

On the other side of the issue, Mr. Rodrieguez had the county tax appraisers on his side, the tourist dollars that would make their way into the economy and the jobs he would create. The sheriff also said the man papa had shot was just grazed and Mr. Rodrieguez would not press charges if papa didn't cause any more trouble. In fact, his lawyer was here to double what he offered papa before. Papa became indignant and told them he would see them in hell.

We walked the trail back to the house in silence, and already the woods seemed changed, like they didn't belong to us, like we were strangers, intruders on our own land. I was sad, but I think mostly I felt that way because of papa. The grief he was suffering was so deep it hurt to see him that way. I wanted to say something, but I didn't know what. At sixteen you can't really comprehend what land means. It was papa's roots, his blood, and sweat and life, and mine, too, but I just didn't realize it.

The first thing papa did when we got back was to go inside the shed to check on his rat traps, leaning the rifle against the wall. A second later the door flung open, papa grabbed the rifle, disappearing back inside. Four rapid shots rang out, then after a pause a fifth one. Papa emerged with his trophy, swinging a bleeding tiger rat by the tail. He suspended the rat on a ten ought fishhook dangling from the buoy line to set an example for any other trespassing rodents. I looked at the swollen body dripping blood, staining the sand, and papa turned to me, smiling for the first time that day, and said she was pregnant.

The tiger rat hung there, stiff and bloated and stinking for days until one morning on our way fishing it was gone. Papa said the wind must have blown it down and a raccoon made off with it, and we didn't talk about it anymore.

As the weeks went by we stuck to our work, fishing and pulling our traps. On the other side of the island, we saw the thousand-foot dock they were building, heard the daily scream of the saws and machinery, breathed the smoke that spilled over and through the trees blowing ashes our way when the wind blew from the west, but we never went back there. Papa complained constantly, swearing, calling it the rape of man, while mama tried to accept it by ignoring it and downplaying papa's warnings to the effects the development would have on the island.

We had just finished smoking some fish when mama said there was a man standing outside, looking nervous by the trail. Papa leaped up, took one look at the suited intruder, and grabbed his carbine. He kicked the screen door open, ran out to the porch yelling, "Them bastards," when I heard a heavy thump on the floor. We scrambled outside. Papa was lying on his stomach, his head turned to the stranger who was now walking hesitantly up to the house. We turned papa over but he was dead, his eyes staring open.

"Is there anything I can do?" the man asked. Mama leaped up and started down the steps screaming, "You bastard, you can get off my property before I shoot you. You've caused my husband to have a heart attack, you greedy bastards!" I grabbed mama, holding on to her tightly. She was shaking uncontrollably.

"You bastards caused this. Trying to pressure papa into selling his land," I told him over mama's shoulder.

"Son, you got me wrong. I'm from the D.N.R. I'm a biologist. I came here to tell you that development on this island isn't going to take place if I have anything to say about it."

Mama stopped shaking as she heard what he said.

"I found the carcass of a particular species of rat, *Oryzomys argentatus*, that we thought was extinct, but apparently it's still alive and breeding on this island. When we finish our studies and confirm what I believe is the only habitat left in the world for this species, I don't think there's a court in this state that's gonna grant building permits."

I couldn't believe what I was hearing. Papa lay at our feet, dead, protecting the land that he loved that was his home. But it was also home to another creature, one that papa hated, and the tiger rat accomplished what papa couldn't.

# HELLO SPRING BREAK

### *ROBIN ORLANDI*

Hello Spring Break
they're writing nasty things about you
in the paper over at Solares Hill,
saying Key West doesn't want you
low class beer-pukers covered in Grateful Dead stickers.
You might ruin our reputation with the rich
who blow Big Bucks.
Who suck down Dom Perignon
and pay five hundred a night for a closet
and two hundred a plate for vichyssoise,
whose high-class wallets wish we would bend
and pretend to be what they want.

Well, it's all a lie;
Key West has been a stink, a stain,
a shrimper, salvage wrecker, scalawag,
cigar-rolling, pool-shooting, dope-smoking,
beatnik, biker, saint, holy harlot flashing her ass
in the face of convention since shipwrecked Spaniards named her,
"Cayo Hueso",
"Bone Key"
por todos los Reys del Sol, Kings of the Sun bleached
skeletons bidding them land on her sacred shores.

Key West ain't no TV show,
Key West ain't a Lexus on Duval Street,
Key West ain't a condo that locks up the waterfront for paying customers
only.
Key West is the wine in a drunken sailor's rowing arms,
Key West is a big fat mama who wants to hug you all,

who plays magic tricks with your mind at night,
who makes you sweat and feeds you,
who leaves you always calling,
calling back to her for more.
Key West is the star of the sea,
who watches over fishermen adrift in liquid night,
she whispers in the artists' ears,
she lights the lamp beside the golden door
por los balseros Cubanos, rafters
willing to die for freedom on these shores.

Freedom. Liberty. Tolerance. Acceptance.
Once upon a time,
everyone you passed on Duval Street would smile and say hello
no one needed two jobs,
or a quarter to park,
or a gold card to spend the night,
or a reservation to touch the sea;
Paradise and free,
but much too much, too tempting,
too much temptation to remain unbitten by the mouth of greed:

INVASION 1973
by men and women wearing suits,
arriving by airplane in the disco decade,
carrying cash
and Robert's Rules of Order,
bent on improving everything,
civilize this backwater island
(faintly reeking of shrimp and sponge)
and maximize her potential to solicit for their bank accounts.
Maximum neon; maximum traffic jam;
Maximum tax; maximum dead reef; maximum rent;
Maximum code enforcement; maximum concrete; maximum t-shirt rip-off;
Maximum fifty dollar boiled lobster with a potato…?
Minimum grouper;
Minimum green space,

Minimum...
ARRGGGHHHH!!!!!
What have they done to this island?
Key West, this is terminal.
They're stealing the waterfront market, the shrimp houses, toxic triangle
tank island, salt ponds, houseboat row
picking over the bones of paradise;
The city need them!
The city's gotta big debt!!
Gotta pay, gotta pay, somebody's gotta pay,
we gotta pay, you gotta pay and pay and pay,
sell your house to the rich man,
sell your johnboat to make room for a Long Island yacht,
build condos from one end of the bridal path to the other,
cover Peary Court in concrete
GIVE IT UP!
GIVE THE RICH MAN A BREAK!
CASTRO IS FALLING!
CASINOS ARE COMING!
THIS WILL BE THE AMERICAN RIVIERA!
IT'S HOPELESS!
So, get your raggedy ass out of our parlour.

AHHH
"...Give us this day our daily bread
and forgive us our trespasses
as we forgive those who trespass against us,
lead us not into temptation, but deliver us from evil."
Can this be forgiven?
Who will raise the waterfront crucified for the sin of poverty?
Should we pray
for the resurrection of local culture?
Hide in Bahama Village?
Hope that the Brandy Group will be kind?
Hemingway's cats laugh and yowl on a decaying fence,
"Doncha get it Bubba?
There's no room left here for the six-toed, the one-eyed,

the mongrel dreamers playing guitar sticks on the sidewalks of paradise",
NO ROOM AT THE INN
for penniless travelers
or their outcast children
seeking the Southern Cross.

Exodus Exodus Exodus
Slip away to the mangers of Stock Island
Where cows and old hippies live in Airstreams,
where midnight waitresses and bicycle mechanics,
bartenders and store clerks,
artists in tin warehouses
Jesus in a shrimp shack
dancers in the alleyways
all plot a resurrection,
a great "rucksack revolution" that quivers over the guava vine.
You heard it here first, listen:
Call up those no class vagabonds,
tell them to come and bring a friend,
Springbreakers and flute-makers,
every pirate in the book:
The Grateful Dead and Wavy Gravy,
Rainbow Children and Earth First!ers, Farmers from Tennessee,
Call the Peace-Eye Bookstore,
The Psychedelic Solution
Saint Mark's Place and Boulder, The Lakota Tribes of Wounded Knee,
Call Mother Teresa, Cesar Chavez, Mahatma Ghandi, Gary Snyder,
Call the Hare Krishna
Call everyone who'd rather sleep in the sand under the stars
than give a nickel to the Hidden Ocean Key Hyatt Zero House.
Tell them to come
and overrun Truman Annex
and stick flowers in the gunbarrels of greed.

# RURAL DELIVERY

## *KIRBY CONGDON*

Dorothy cut the crusts off the sandwiches with a sharp knife. Her arm moved in a see-saw motion as she trimmed each slice. Now and then she cut off a piece of lettuce that stuck out, or quickly pushed it back into place. Looking accusingly at the clock, she saw there was time. As the knife cut the seconds in two, the back door opened slowly.

"Hurry up," Dorothy said. "The wind's blowing."

"Sorry," her husband, Ray, answered. He stood by the door a moment. A letter hung from his hand.

"Letter," he said.

"I see it," Dorothy replied without looking up.

"I guess it's for you," he suggested.

"I guess it is." Dorothy cut a stubborn end of bread away.

The knife scraped against the table top as she brushed the crumbs into a pile and tumbled the heap over the edge of the table into the cup of her hand. Ray held out the letter to her.

Dorothy's eyes shot up and looked her husband full in the face, and then away, as if in embarrassment. "My hands are full," she explained. "Who's it from?"

"Edna."

Dorothy wiped her hands on her apron and pretended to laugh a little. Ray put the letter under an ashtray next to an old postal card from the Riviera.

On the envelope Edna's familiar flourish displayed itself. "Edna!" Dorothy thought. Her comings and goings! The things she said! And her own crowd, the late middle-aged "gang" that made up the Ladies' Aid down in Key West were so bland, like those pictures of the Mediterranean with that deadly blue sea and thick, dry foliage on the hills that looked, in their distance, as flat as Florida.

She was glad her own life, while it wasn't any more exciting than those of her friends in town, and certainly less exciting than Edna's, wasn't lost in its own pattern. But Ray's was. That was the real trouble. Oh, it wouldn't be another man. Not at her age, but, well, Edna was full of ideas. She would have some when she got back to New York again.

Dorothy pulled out the letter from under the ashtray and gave the postal card a shove until it was out of sight. It was as though the color of those washed-out hills had run and spoiled the water. Oceans should be alive and changing, begging you to come out to the unknown. The unknown appealed to her because she wanted to understand everything, to have done everything. When Dorothy looked up, Ray stood there empty-handed.

"I haven't got time to make supper. You know that, don't you, Ray? I'm late with these sandwiches for the Ladies' Aid as it is." She knew it wasn't true, but it soon would be if she delayed. To prove her statement, she declared, "I'll have to get some soup on the way back. There's so little time."

"What kind do you want?" Dorothy stopped in the middle of the doorway. Her tongue fussed with a lettuce leaf caught between her teeth.

"It doesn't matter." Ray sat down sideways. His wife stepped over, picked up a plate of sandwiches and set it down before him.

"This'll have to do till I get back. Vegetable, chicken, noodle, or what?" she insisted. Ray dragged the sandwich plate nearer, and answered without looking up. "Oh, vegetable's all right." He took a bite of his sandwich.

"Well! There's no point in buying what's 'all right.' I've cashed the Social Security checks. What kind do you want?"

"Vegetable," Ray mumbled, feigning interest. Dorothy left the room hurriedly. Then realizing that she had let herself be overcome with temper, she called back, "There's coffee on the stove."

Before sitting down at the little dining table, she faced the empty doorway and called back to the kitchen again. "Cream's in the icebox." She listened for the sound of the latch, and hearing it, leaned an elbow on the table, pushed herself almost absent-mindedly into a chair, and opened the letter. She laid it out flat on the table top, and ironed the wrinkles and creases out with the palm of her hand.

"Dear Dot," the letter began, and ended, "P.S. Are you coming up north here? There are plenty of jobs but the youngsters get them all. We'd need time to find something you would like."

When Dorothy folded the letter up, Ray was sitting in the old Morris chair, thumbing through a fishing catalog. Dorothy stood up, walked to the window and folded her arms. She hadn't been up to Miami for two years, and how long was it since she had been in New York? It would be natural for her to go now. Yes! she would! She lifted her head, emancipated, and turned around to face her new life. Ray was still sitting in his chair. The insteps of his shoes were muddy, but she let it go. Looking out the window again, she declared, "Edna's asked me up." She paused briefly. "I think I'll go." Her voice seemed to shout in her own ears. She heard Ray's magazine fall into his lap. Before he could speak, she added, "I haven't answered yet." She pressed a thumb into the soil of a window plant. The facts were given. The danger was past. She was going, but she hadn't really said so. So there was nothing to discuss. She went out into the kitchen, leaving all discussion behind her, sitting in the Morris chair. She expected him to call, though. Sometimes he was surprisingly direct. She hastily poured water loudly from the tap into a metal pitcher to drown out the voice she might hear. Holding tightly onto the handle of the pitcher, she returned to the dining table and stepped nonchalantly to the window. There, she busied herself with watering the plant until the pot leaked at the bottom and spilled onto its window sill. A little embarrassed at her inefficiency, she apologized and lifted the pitcher, wiping off a drop that hung on it. "I guess it didn't need that much," and smiled a little. She had to say something else because Ray was still silent. His side of the room was a ragged hole opening onto the void. She had to fill it up with something. "I never could measure liquids—not by sight."

"I never saw you measure anything when you cook, Dotty, but it always comes out right, don't it? You don't follow no directions, do you?"

"No," Dorothy said, hardly moving her lips. His compliments always threw her off balance, even when he used the double negative. She began again. "I'd better tell Edna I'll be coming."

"Okay," he said. "The place won't go to pieces. And I've got the boat to go to if it does!"

"This place?" she thought. "What does this place, or the boat have to do with it?"

She wiped the water on the window sill with the corner of her apron. When she looked at Ray again, in as casual a manner as she could, he was engrossed in the catalog. Dorothy pulled writing materials out of a drawer noisily, leaving the pitcher on the window sill. She arranged the ink and paper neatly on the table. She looked back at the pitcher, half expecting it to, somehow, leak. When it didn't she took a breath. As she spoke, her voice was distinct now. She faced him. "I don't know how long I'll be gone," she warned, but Ray only answered, "Why, stay as long as you're invited," and turned a page. Holding her pen poised above the paper like a weapon, she waited for him to go on, but he only dropped the catalog again, threw his head back and closed his eyes.

Finished, Dorothy stuck her letter into an envelope and sealed it. "Have you got a stamp? Never mind. I'll find one." She couldn't make him put the stamp of approval on his own future like that. Nor, she realized, as she scrutinized his defenseless face, could she ask him to mail it. This was her responsibility and she'd do that herself. She wondered if she could catch the outgoing mail in Key West on her way to the Ladies' Aid. She looked for a stamp in her pocketbook. There was none. Nor were there any in the desk. She would look in the dashboard of the car. Anyway, she thought, picking up the car keys, the post office is still open.

She left the house as softly as a robber, and, lest the motor should wake Ray up, she let the car coast down the slight incline of the driveway until she had gotten a little distance from the house. She swung the car around into the road that went across the causeway into town. Now, as she put the car into gear, she felt wicked. This is the first step, she thought. Then she knew, before she left, before she committed herself, she would have to tell him clearly that she would be leaving him alone. And for a long time. Perhaps for always. What would he say? It would destroy him. His little world of habit and daily pattern would have to be completely readjusted, but wouldn't he see, after a while, when he had gotten over it, that she needed more out of life than he could provide? He would have to see it. After all, even with her strength of character, it was going to be as great a change for her as it would be for him. She had her adjustments to make too, enormous ones. Somehow, he would learn to survive his, just as she herself would learn—with Edna's help—to survive hers.

Dorothy followed the road down toward town. The Gulf of Mexico on one side and the Atlantic Ocean on the other were green and reflected the light of the sky, which hung down like a newly-laundered table cloth put out to dry. The flamboyant edges of the tropical trees stood up against it as sharply as petticoat lace that had been freshly ironed. Dorothy felt a deep breath of satisfaction fill her lungs as though she herself had supplied the essential, correct pressure on the iron that had flattened out the branches of these trees on the sky, so still, clean and unmoving. The landscape was a printed picture, and the road ran into it carrying Dorothy along. She held onto the steering wheel lightly. She was relaxed because she was busy without really doing anything. The motion of the car permeated her being and lulled her mind into a quaking kind of peace. The wheels automatically followed the few gentle twists in the road until the first commercial buildings and hotels jumped into sight.

In her heart she was reluctant to arrive so quickly, but the car, somehow, didn't slow down. She had already passed the Matthews' house. Then came the Peterson place, Margie Dixon's house and the old Slavinski store. Did she need anything at the shopping mall while she was here?

"I should have taken the grocery list. We're already out of butter. That's habit for you," she thought. "You never think; just act — even in emergencies, like that time when I was sick and Ray ran the house alone."

Here she was going to the post office as she did most any day, but this time an important turning point in a lifetime could be folded in an envelope and sent on its way at the cost of a stamp. It was so easy!

The gang at the Ladies' Aid would take the news with astonishment. But she would be calm and indifferent about it, accepting it quietly, firmly. They would admire her a little, Dorothy reflected. How could she leave them, the Ladies' Club, her friends, the climate and all, they would ask. "Everything's so easy for you!" Then she would politely deny it, confident in their belief! She would shrug a shoulder perhaps and say, "It only takes a letter and the price of a stamp at the post office." But now a frown broke Dorothy's brow. She had forgotten the letter.

There would be no time now to go back and be on time for the Ladies' Aid, too. Her drama was spoiled. She would have to put off going to the post office. She drove on to the Parish House where the gang met. She decided she would let them think the letter had gone off. She would still be going, wouldn't she? And if she did change her mind after all, and if someone asked—next week perhaps? she would explain the delay—how she couldn't really just abruptly leave Ray alone—for his sake.

Dorothy rehearsed a sigh to herself as she gained speed down the street. The sigh would mean that Ray tied her down so, but, being a woman of some decision, she could still make up her own mind. She stepped on the gas. It really was time to be getting along. If she didn't hurry, the meeting would already have begun and she would be too late to tell them the news. She smiled. To the rest of the gang, the invitation to go to New York and work would be like a call from the unknown. She would tell them that, dull as he is, Ray had said that the house—and their boat—would not go to pieces so that she could feel comfortable and free about going, and about having a new interest, about starting a new life, about— But she knew, now, that, of course the house would deteriorate. The plants would probably die in the first hot spell. Who would take care of the house properly? Was she obligated to stay, then?

Yes. It would be her sacrifice. Looking at her watch, she realized the post office would now be closed. She almost said it out loud: "—and it's closed, closed!—till Monday!"

# AND SHE DIALED 0

## *JUDY ADAMS*

In the shallow warm turquoise waters and deep cool watered docks, the tide of season in full flood deposits travelers, many to stay when the tide retreats, to call Key West home. I am one of these, a woman of 41, riding a bike I can hardly balance. I love to wear the vivid, strong-scented flowers abundant here in my frizzy hair. I am powerfully drawn to others with their own variations upon the theme of being oneself. I love the feel of the wind on my body and to look openly into other faces, to smile and to weep. I like to examine what the tide has left on our shores at Mallory Square at sunset.

When I was a farm girl, I believed the claim that if you waited at a certain sidewalk café in Paris long enough, everyone in the world worth seeing would pass by. I never stayed there long enough to see them all or have my presence noted. I have sobbed into foreign telephones from excess relief that anyone is still alive at home to answer the telephone call from me, searching the earth for the release from the past. I want those at home to be there when I am ready to return to their world that I know so well.

Here on an old concrete dock on the northwest side of Key West, often I have stayed until midnight in the summers, to catch breezes and to listen to the musicians. During the full moon we have made up parties to howl at the moon. This always begins in a spirit of jest and affectionate ridicule at our own interest in astrology and ends with serious baying.

Sitting on the concrete platform and eating, I admire the cloud formations that are beginning to reflect and hold the various colors we have all come here to watch. Many come for the first time. Others could set a watch at the half-hour before sunset, so long had they been drawn by the glow in the western sky. I am one of those. I could watch the sky from my boat deck home, as I do the sunrise, but I am a treasure hunter, too.

The music tonight in front of the platform is a group of drum and flute players. They have the best spot, it is highly sought. These people play from love and joy of life and to supplement their food stamps with this income. Those that need the most, get it. In this case, it is the seated drummer. He has a wife and a new baby that I now sit talking to. The baby is curled and sleeping against his radiant mother's filling breast. Her stomach is pouching like she is five-months pregnant and not yet the mother of her second child. She is full of her recent drama.

"I want to call my mother, I want to talk to her so bad, I have been trying to get in touch with her all day."

A public phone, that has no doors to close, stands near and she goes to it and dials 0.

"Yes operator, I want to make a collect call to Cherry Valley, Ohio. This is Mary Lou calling. Hello, Mother, it is me, Mary Lou. I am in Key West. Yes, I still love it here. We wanted the baby to be born here. The positive vibrations are powerful. He will need all he can get in this world. Yes, I am fine, I am so happy. Oh, Mother, I have been waiting all day to tell you about it. Oh, I know it is a long drive into Cleveland . . . Say hello to Aunt Millie for me. Has she left yet? Well, give her my love. Let me tell you about . . . Yes, I know it is my second, but it was different this time. I had him at home with a midwife and friends. Rene really delivered him. I wish you could have seen him, he was the most beautiful I have ever seen a man. He was so open, I mean totally and completely open to me and the universe, you know what I mean? Well, his nose, I swear it was flared like a running horse's! I could see into his soul.

"I am fine. I am here at sunset. Rene is playing the drums. He earns money doing it, Mother, and tonight is a special night. I need to talk to you now, I don't know if I can write all this. We are going to call him the Morning Star. He is 7 pounds, 3 1/4 ounces and 22 1/4 inches long, and so perfect. Long fingers and not much hair, just a little, like a man who has lost all but that little ridge from ear to ear. I expected lots of curls, too. It is easy to imagine the dogwoods, the trees are covered with orange blossoms, not the fruit, but hundreds of flowers shaped like orchids, but brilliant orange. But let me tell you about us and all of us having Morning Star. Yes, we had her with us to watch. Oh Mother, you should have heard her, when I was sitting on the pail to pass the afterbirth . . . Wait, let me tell you, I can't relate to this disgusting you. Well, I know she wasn't, she was interested. Remember how we used to bother poor old Sylvia when she was having her kittens, lifting up her leg and peering? Kids are interested.

"Well, Mother, I don't agree. I don't want to argue and make each other feel bad, I love you. Yes, I wanted so much all day to tell you. I have felt so close to you all day, and now that we are speaking the feeling is, is . . . Please don't cry . . . yes, cry if you feel like crying. Who am I to tell you what or how to feel? Want to say hello to Patty? She is right by . . . I understand. So will she, I think. I'll just tell her you are crying because you are so happy. I hope you are? I don't know where everything went that I was going to tell you, it was all so beautiful. Yes, I am still selling sprouts and tofu. No, send me some money instead. I don't think we are coming to visit soon. I *am* home. Good bye . . . Yes, I'll write all about it. There is someone waiting for the phone. Good bye."

My young friend hangs up the phone and turns away and then walks a few feet and sits upon the concrete curb at the water's edge and stares at the tree-covered island the sun is directly above. A little girl sits next to her, touching, silent.

A young man in cut-off shorts and a military hair cut and trim face hair feeds quarters into the phone.

"Hello, Bobby this is Stu, I am in Key West. Can you believe this? A whole bunch of people are playing music and dancing and eating green slop out of a bucket while the sun sets. They do it every night. Listen, I want you to bring my car down and yourself for a weekend, you'll love it. This ain't Texas. Green, greeeeen and clear water. Free and easy, Happy Hour almost all day. Street full of fags to kick the shit out of, you'll love it. Chicks? Foxes, foxes and all of them loose and free, don't hardly wear any clothes. Come on! Bring the car, you can get work here. You're right, ain't nothing for you in that town. Come on down here and we'll kick asses and get more than we can handle. Okay, look for me at the base. Wait 'til you see this place. I swear, not six feet from here a lady like I was telling you about is doing a belly dance. I ain't lying . . . don't you hear the music? The way she rolls and swings gives me lots to think about at night. Of course I'm getting plenty, but I do have some time alone, on duty any way. Yeah, I been drinking, but I am watching this guy swallowing fire, damnation, and he is spitting it out too, like a dragon, maybe eight feet. Okay, operator. Okay Bobby, see you here soon . . . careful of my car. Bye."

When the operator calls back with time and charges, the boy-man answers and then leaves the phone dangling off the hook. He joins six other young men who look like him in dress and hair; they stand around drinking from cans wrapped in insulating foam. Another young man stops to warn them not to drink in public and they move to the far end of the pier.

The phone is replaced on the hook by a thin young woman in pink shorts and a T-shirt. She turns to walk away, stops and returns to the phone. She dials 0.

"Operator, I want to make a collect call to Santa Monica, California . . . Yes, I'll wait."

The woman is a little unsteady on her feet, as her eyes search the crowd. A man with flowing blonde hair and purple yoga pants clinging to his thin hips gives her a warm smile and comes closer with his wares of pins twisted from wire that, before your eyes as you wait, turn into any name or saying you wish. Most are only four dollars. He supports his family and occasionally picks up a job to make a fine piece of jewelry, a sample of which he wears around his neck. His little girl is dancing in front of the group of musicians, easily and in rhythm. Another child her age, already losing touch with that part of herself, also dances, sometimes in rhythm, mostly not. Unlike the unsmiling adults who dance, they open their mouths to the evening breezes and stop to jump up and down in delight with themselves. The woman in pink looks at his samples blankly, running her fingers over them but not really seeing. He has come close, not to try to sell her, but to soothe her obvious distress. Her hands shake and she stutters into the phone, "I want to call collect. This is Paula. I'll talk to anyone . . . Hi Dad. Yes, I am fine. I'm still in Key West. I don't have my purse with me. I'm sorry about the collect call. No, I'll pay you back. Oh, I just wanted to talk. Really, everything is fine. The people are great, I have made a lot of friends. Well, I am broke, and I was wondering . . . Oh, I hate to ask . . . Please don't tell Mom. No, I don't want it if she knows. Daddy, please. Well, it's expensive here, and I have been eating out, and well, some people, I have been paying for their drinks and well, I am broke. I don't want to leave just yet, I want to travel. I have a friend I'm going with. He has traveled a lot. Yes, I guess he was married once. I don't know his life history, and I don't care. I am not yelling, I am sorry if I sounded like I was . . . That? It's a man blowing a conch shell. No, I haven't drunk any rum out of one yet.

"Listen, Dad, this call is going to cost a lot. Sure you don't mind? Well, I have been kind of camping out the last few days, nights . . . .I mean, the weather is wonderful here, it doesn't get cold at night ever, like in California. Well, if you'll send me the money, I want to go down to Jamaica with my friend. We might get a ride on a boat. Oh, we'd swim and lay on the beach. Yes, I know we can do that here, but I've never been to another country. Are you going to send me the money? Two thousand dollars. How soon can you send it? Please don't tell Mom, she wouldn't understand. I love him. I said, I love him. I'll talk into the phone better. All I know is that I am happy with him and we are going to travel. What does it matter what his name is? I am a grown woman now, I am over 30. I said, I am going to hang up now. Oh, send it to Western Union. I'll find it, it's a small town, I walk everywhere. I'll write to you from Jamaica. I've been kinda having too much fun to write, the days slip by somehow. Now it is sunset and the sky is every color but blood red, like LA. I guess the air is clean here, like the water. Don't worry, I am not rushing into anything . . . Do I have to? Sure, she just came in? Hello, Mom. Yeah, I have been having a great time. No, Mother, I have not forgotten, I'll never forget the accident. It is the first thing I see in my eyes in the morning and the last at night . . . Well, you asked . . . Time has passed and I am still alive . . . Yes, I am a little drunk. I have come from a bar and we had drinks. It's called 'Happy Hour' and thousands of other people do it with me. This is a really very cultured place. Right now I can see four groups of people singing and playing instruments. They are artists . . . A lot of them work in the clubs in town. I guess they just like to enjoy music.

"There is a man with two green lizards wrapped around his neck, he looks just like one of his pets, a six-foot freckled lizard. You can see him in a movie, it just came out, something about Castro. Made here. I haven't seen it. And I see two jugglers, one is juggling knives while the other lights up some metal sticks . . . How could I make all this up? I am just telling you what I can see . . . Put Dad back on a minute. Good bye . . . Hello Dad, you'll do that for me? I love you and thanks."

She hangs up the phone and stands with her head bowed a moment and walks over to a group of men that lie on the cement, wearing the only clothes they own, all of them needing a bath for the last week.

One shakes another sleeping and warns him, "You had better look awake if you want to stay out of jail. The fuzz are here."

They take the common bottle wrapped in a brown bag and put it out of sight for now. Later they will meet on Caroline Street and pass the evening sitting on the porch of the place once known as the Bucket of Blood. I see them any hour of the day or night as I pass from the boat dock to Duval Street. I always wondered where their ladies came from. I wonder how long the lady in pink will be with them? The young man with the twisted wire art and I catch each other's eye and he comes over.

"Beautiful sky tonight, the colors are changing so fast. I think I like it like this, subtle, not a Las Vegas of the sunsets. There was a wedding last night."

"Here?"

"Way down on the end. I could have died from the pleasure. A ski boat with a parachute rider went madly back and forth behind them. It was almost like getting married at the circus. True, I thought, it was life in full celebration of itself."

"Yes, this is a celebration of life. Remember when the holy rollers used to come down on Friday night and revile us as evil sun worshippers? They too were all a part of life, yeah? I thought your parents were here."

"They are. They are in their car."

"At sunset?"

"My Dad has his .38 and my Mom a can of mace."

"You are putting me on."

"God's truth."

"Your parents?"

"My very own. They are in a beige sedan."

"Right, I saw them."

"They are your age, you know."

"Too bad."

"I know."

I see another friend careen her bike across the lot. She has on her dancing clothes and flowers woven into her braids. Her dog is sitting in a milk crate wired to the handle bars. He has flowers attached with rubber bands to his head. A real ugly mutt, he has barely any hair since his loving mistress is a veggie and insists he be one too. He sits without whining when she leaves him in the basket and hurries to the pay phone. She stands guarding it and when it rings she grabs it.

"Yes, Mother, this is Bebe," says the person we know as Sun Maiden. "Sorry I couldn't get to Sloppy Joe's in time for your call. I've been at the beach all day, getting energy . . . Well, what is it? The sun is almost down and I want to get its last energy for the night . . . What? . . . What! No. You aren't joking, are you? Alright, let me breathe and think a minute . . . When did this happen? . . . He could not have killed himself! . . . I don't care! I don't believe it! I'll never believe it! . . . Are you okay? . . . You want me to come up there or what? . . . I can hitch out . . . Send me the plane ticket if you will be happier . . . No one is going to hurt me. I have done it thousands of times . . .

Okay, for you I'll wait, but I could be there by morning if I left now . . . Oh, you have reservations on the last flight? . . . See you at the airport . . . Got to find someone to watch the dog. Oh, what am I babbling about? I'll be there. You just hold on until I get there. I love you and Jack loved you. He really isn't gone. Oh, I hope this is all a dream. His soul will be so disturbed if he was murdered . . . We'll think what to do when I get there . . . Good bye."

She walks to the end of the pier and sits with thumb and forefinger touching, circling, and draws deep breaths as the sun flames its last few seconds in today's sky. A friend approaches with a guitar, hoping to have her take it and rock us all. She looks at him blankly, scrambles to her feet, not with her usual gracefulness.

She says to the sun, "I don't believe he would die and not tell me about it, my own brother. I have to go talk to him about this. I know he will give me a sign."

She takes the shaggy mutt over to her friend with the new baby. They speak a moment, each reluctant to intrude their feelings, this day so different, upon each other. The little girl hugs the dog with abandon and takes him into the circle to dance with her. The crowd laughs. The dog smiles at them.

A girl that looks like she could have stepped out of an advertisement in any American magazine, as a perfect example of what a woman should look like and wear, approaches the phone cautiously and looks about to see who is watching her. She removes the credit card from her purse and makes a call to her parents on a card that she has "borrowed." She cannot bring herself to call collect and she has no money. The drummers have stopped for the moment and another group of players fill the souls around with American bluegrass, played by well trained musicians who live to make music.

One of them told me how his father bitterly complained to him once, "Hell, I could play like that too, if I spent all day long stoned and playing music like you do."

He overlooked that he did not want to and his son did. A couple in blue jeans improvise a jig and other foot work they've seen in Roy Rogers movies.

"Hello Mom, it's me, Kelly. I am in Key West . . . Oh, this is really a beautiful town . . . Oh, I got off that yacht . . . the captain was a jerk. You know, who needs the hassle . . . Well, I have a great place here, the houses are really old and the trees are big. I have a really great job at this fine restaurant. They are going to make me manager, I am making about sixty dollars a night in tips . . . I don't know when I'll be manager, but I know it will pay a lot more. This is a really busy place, you can hear it . . . Huh? We sure pack them in . . . Oh, I am on a break, I wanted to call now because of the time difference, you know, let you know I am fine and got here safe. I lost my clothes, could you send me some? . . . Oh, how about General Delivery? I might move in a few days. I am going to do some modeling, too. A guy came up to me on the beach and wanted to take some pictures of me. I am going to make seventy-five dollars an hour. Oh, I know I am going to love it here and you are going to be so proud of me . . . Oh, that sound? It's someone blowing on a conch shell. It is a tradition here, when Happy Hour starts or closes . . . I am going to get so blond from all this sun . . . No, I am not putting bleach on it . . . I am not. I am taking care of it . . . Well, I just wanted to say hello. The zip here is 33040 . . .Remember, General Delivery. I love you too, Mom. Maybe I can buy you a plane ticket soon to come and visit me . . . Don't worry, I am doing real good. Good-bye."

Furtively, she puts the card in her purse, removes it again and starts to the trash with it. Her friend, who's been listening to the conversation, takes it.

"Are you crazy? We may need this. Now, let's go see who we can find to buy us dinner."

A grey haired man in denim and tattoos, his hair in a grizzled ponytail skewered with a roach clip, is waiting for his collect call to be accepted. He answers with, "Guess who this is, go on guess. . . . Yeah, well there is something I want you to hear." He takes the phone and holds it as close as he can to the music, high in the air, as if it is a camera. He stands beaming in approval of the music, the dancers, the breeze, and his cleverness at thinking to turn on the folks back home.

After a few minutes of this he says into the mouth piece, "Ain't that beautiful, ain't that something? This is all going on right now, all of us having a party to watch the sun go down. It is sitting on top of an oil tank now . . . Wait, we are going to see the Green Flash! . . . wait . . . wait . . . just a minute! . . . Well, it didn't happen tonight. Oh well, I just wanted to share this with you all.. . . The clapping is for the sun . . . Yeah, clapping for the sun! What a way to live! . . . I know you have a sunset in Tennessee, but nobody claps."

# SMALL CRAFT WARNINGS

*DANNE HUGHES*

you see it first from the air
sheets of turquoise stained by reef
mangrove shadows seagrass sand
the dream spread flat as paint
channels inking azure flats
nothing no one odd lone boat


then cayo hueso isle of bones
thick with pastel wooden houses
church spires cycads palms giant hardwoods
libertine perfumes pull you down
into solandra jasmine ylang ylang ram's horn
datura lantana frangipani key lime &
old cuttings from dead seamen run amok


you have arrived at the southernmost dream
where an inch means a yard in paradise
you are staying here
pinned by currents fiercer than
the river Gulf Stream charging north offshore
to dream here in a doll's house
on a plot of land no bigger than a finger

in this dream you will watch your hands
pluck mangoes reach for starfruit and
bananas hanging heavy in the yard
where papaya ackee sour orange sugar apple
swell in pregnant trees

you will stay awhile

# Small Craft Warnings

on your road to nowhere else

sheets of rain drum tin roofs
drench you in your dreams
seep through coral out to sea
you've seen the world you'll dream on here
of tree frogs lizards cats and ghekkoes
scarlet-throated in pandanus leaves
above monstrous caverns made of roots
crimson claws spike bare limbs
waterspouts spin offshore

       and

there are small craft warnings

small craft should exercise caution
hunker down
settle in silt
list in port under winds
which can smash them to shards
on hard corals

there are small craft advisories
small craft should exercise caution
but you think you've found safe haven on this rock
and you want to dream your dream
float above that hairline crack
between survival and fat takings
old ghosts whisper nothing's changed

small craft had best seek shelter
but you like me take off
ignore all signs just dive right in
and we're lost out on blue water

small craft warnings pierce the night

which light can you trust
of the beacons flashing out to sea
to guide you into port?
red right return
red right return
blink the dark channels

small craft warnings pierce the night
as your dream races out with the tide

your life is all at sea
the dream in jigsaw puzzle pieces
town is ripping at the seams
where are the lit markers to bring you back
to somewhere you call home?

it's red right return
down the dark channels
stars in your eyes
& blood on the water
down the dark passage to home

# ARMANDO, SCULPTOR

## *ALLEN MEECE*

Back in the days when Caroline Street was part of a working seaport, people there seemed, only seemed, to drink more than they worked. The winos saw me sleeping in the car at Miss T's Raw Bar and felt empathetic. I was doing ok, it was better than living with the wolf constantly at my front door in Rochester, Rotten Chester we called it. Finally I ran out the back door and didn't stop running until the road stopped in the Gulf of Mexico. You can't die here, or even get miserable, in winter.

Two winos came over and held out a grocery bag with a homey motto printed on it, "It's more than a grocery store, it's a social center."

"You want some pot? Have some pot."

I was astounded by what I saw — five or six inches of dark green leafy matter in the bottom of the bag. These "dirtbags," as prissy people called them, were walking around with thousands of dollars-worth of smoking material in a brown paper grocery bag.

"I can have some, free?" I asked.

"Sure, take some."

I reached in, took a small handful and looked up to see if they minded the quantity. They didn't. I took a bigger handful and put it between the sheets of a yellowed newspaper in the back seat.

Somebody must've made a successful run and scored a bale. Their ship came in. Weeks of joyful living were in the bag. They wanted to share, give some away, pay back society for all the spare change they'd begged on Caroline Street.

It was too much for me. I was committed to beer and didn't want another habit. I took the vegetable matter to Armando, a sculptor whom I'd met on the dock at sunset where he sold his bronzes. I wasn't sure the pot would be good for him. They said he tried to make engines run on water.

That's why I took it to him, I needed a good laugh. He was living near Eaton and White in an eight-by-ten room with attached bathroom. I remember when he lived illegally in a closet-sized artist's studio. It was rented

# Armando, Sculptor

cheaply as a work space but Armando unfolded a cot every night and put two plastic jugs under it; one for drinking water and one for urine. Risky.

I remember when he had a little box trailer and tried to sleep in the parking lot. Drunken tourists, returning to their cars after midnight, were rowdy and noisy and Armando didn't sleep well there.

The trailer's license plate made it legal to be somewhere at night time, the sleeping hours. They didn't issue such plates to the homeless. You admired his attempt at independence in the narrow box on wheels.

His new room cost thirty dollars a week. Today, the same place, fixed up a little, is a motel room going for fifty bucks a night. Some people still don't know what causes homelessness. They blame it on lack of character. Shit. It's their own lack of character that causes it, brushing people aside like flies in their greedy pursuit of real estate profits.

Having a room with a bathroom was quite a step up in the world. It meant Armando was a functioning, independent man. He even entertained women there.

Armando's stuff matched the cubic capacity of the room. Tall acetylene and oxygen bottles stood around the bathroom commode. One cylinder had toppled over and cracked the toilet which was semi-repaired with strips of duct tape. The owner would've kicked him out if he knew Armando broke the stool and couldn't buy a new one. The tape was unpeeling and the porcelain buddha was dribbling into the living room, a room stuffed with all the equipment necessary to sculpt bronze for a living while developing an invention of a hydrogen-powered boat engine/water pump.

When Armando let me in, he was sweating and holding a hammer and chisel in one hand. He'd been chiselling a seam in the cracked floor tiles to channel water out the front door. The mind of a genius.

At the foot of the bed was a table supporting a tub of water containing a clear plexiglass engine, a prototype that Armando called "El Pulpo," The Octopus. It was his ticket out of the dumps and into the stratosphere of respectable living where he belonged.

The invention was connected by wires to a car battery on the floor that was hooked-up to a battery charger that was plugged into an electrical fixture on the wall that fed a fan, worklight, hotplate, radio and assorted gadgets that only Armando understood.

You respected the women who spent the evening here. You really respected Armando for attracting them here. The way he talked, they were attractive women

118

who were just tired of the lifestyles of the guys up north. Some kind of stud.

He cleared space on the bed and we sat down and fired-up the gift I'd brought.

"Did you hear back from General Motors about your invention?" I asked.

"Ahh, my aing-bang-shion," he said in Cubanese.

"An engineer wrote to me and said they want to study it but he thinks it uses too much electricity for boats. They only know what they learn in school, they do not know how to look at new things."

"Did you ever calculate how much power it takes from the wall against how much power it puts out?"

"That would take an hour to test and I cannot get El Pulpo to run more than three to five seconds. Besides, I don't think the manager would like me to run an engine in my room," he said with glee at the commotion it would raise.

"I just want to sell my idea for getting clean power from the hydrogen in water. You know, the only by-product of my engine is water vapor?"

"Great, a marine engine that doesn't use gas or oil."

"Yes, it definitely is a great aing-bang-shion."

He connected the battery charger to a radio that was lying in pieces on the table and music came from a speaker somewhere amid the jumble.

The music seemed good and the smoke felt good. We decided that nothing would be more enjoyable than to watch El Pulpo work out.

"The battery is charged and ready to go," said Armando. "I found a good switch yesterday on a broken moped and I don't have to twist the wires together to make it run."

He flipped the switch and a little sizzling noise began. Bubbles of hydrogen out-gassed from the water and floated to the top of the combustion chamber. Armando fiddled with the circuits and the pocket of hydrogen grew larger than optimum. The engine went "BANG!" and blew a quart of water onto the floor.

He fumbled with some wires and pulled then apart before it could happen again.

"Wow!" I said, laughing both at him and with him, "that's powerful."

Shaken, but laughing with pride, he said, "The next model, I will be able to control the amount of hydrogen in the cylinder."

He noticed something wrong in the engine and lifted it from the tank.

"The seams are broken by the explosion. I must begin my next model today. Hand me that screwdriver please."

I watched him disassemble his dream, and left, wishing him good luck. I was skeptical about boat engines that had to be plugged into the wall but said nothing to dampen his enthusiasm. In our kind of life, spirit was all that kept you going.

That night the cops raided my car.

Blaring whoop, whoop, whoops. A high-intensity searchlight piercing the car windows above where I lay on the front seat. A second car pulls up and does the same thing, like coming to a robbery. Their radios are turned up until the cars sound like robo-women. That scares perpetrators who had mean mothers and is the cops' form of war chant and gets them excited for the job they have to do.

I knew what it was, I'd been rousted before. But two cars and three cops was a bit much. It turned out they had a bona fide citizen's complaint about me, this wasn't routine harassment.

Identification card and answers. While one's writing a ticket for "sleeping in public," another gingerly pulls the door handle and the door swings open as if by magic. They shine flashlights in the back and conduct an illegal search but who are you going to call? The cops?

Their excitement dies down when they see there's not much here but a guy sleeping. One hands me a ticket and they leave. They know my car so I don't bother trying to sleep in it somewhere else. I get out and walk to the salt ponds to finish sleeping.

I'd spent months out there under the bright stars with the casuarinas whispering in the wind. Like other oppressed people I found sanctuary among the trees. They're alive. They hide you and they leave you alone. It's not just a coincidence that the world is being deforested. There's something big behind those axes.

But you can't keep your stuff in the woods. You can exist happily and sanely but you can't get the power to defend yourself. I got a car for keeping stuff and sleeping. I bought it for fifteen dollars a week for ten weeks out of my dishwashing pay.

The city's penalty is seventy-five dollars each time you get caught sleeping outside. Not each night, each time. You could get caught many times a night if you weren't a disappearing Houdini. The city provides no shelters for its own homeless citizens. The good burghers don't say it out loud but the message is clear — if you're broke, leave.

I didn't see criminal intent in my being broke and sleepy. I'm not going to trudge the country looking for sleep. I fought for this country and presumably that included the Coral City. If I now have to fight at home for what I was protecting over there, I will.

I pled not guilty.

They gave me a negotiator with the misnomer, "public defender."

I told him the no sleeping law discriminates against poor people and he should defend me on constitutional grounds.

He refused, said he'd defend me on the facts.

I told him the facts were the cops couldn't say I was sleeping because their lights and noises woke me up before they could see me in the car.

When he relayed this fact to the prosecution, they changed the offense to "living in a vehicle."

"That's absurd. There was no food or clothes or stove in the car. This is dirty pool. How am I supposed to mount a defense if they keep changing the charge?"

"They're allowed to do that up to thirty days before trial."

He already knew what I was just learning; the little guy isn't supposed to mount any defense.

"Well, the hell with that. You're going to defend me on civil liberty grounds. Then it doesn't matter what discriminatory charge they use. I'll get it into the Supreme Court if it takes me the rest of my life!"

And then my so-called attorney, my ally, my friend in the courtroom said, "Don't try to use the court for political reform. Demonstrate in front of city hall or pass out leaflets or something."

"This ain't no political reform movement. This is defending my ass from the law. I want a new lawyer."

He hemmed and hawed and stalled and a few days later came back with an offer to drop my fine to thirty dollars.

"Nope," I said, "I'm not guilty and I'm not paying thirty dollars to say 'no contest' to the charges, whatever they may be today."

Finally he couldn't hide from the situation and said he'd defend me factually and appeal on constitutional grounds if I lost.

"Sometimes the cops don't show up," he said, displaying his utter lack of confidence in his courtroom ability, which I sort of expected. I think the truth is that the prosecutor tells the cops not to show up when the law is bad and the defendant knows it. If one person beats a bad law then everyone can do it and they'd have to devise another bad law to take away peoples' rights.

On the morning that I picked a jury, one potential juror raised his hand and asked, "Your honor, am I to understand that this man is going to trial for sleeping in a car?"

"That's right," was all the judge could say.

Only three jurors showed up trial the next day. While we waited to see if more would straggle in, the prosecutor offered to drop the fine if only I'd cave in.

"Nope, I want this law to be tried. I don't think it'll pass muster."

"Court dismissed," said the judge.

The prosecutor threw in the towel after throwing thousands of state dollars against me. I was a winner at last. Thank you, Florida. I was joyful but not that happy. The law left me alone but it's still out there shaking the bushes at night for the homeless — my people, your people, Americans.

While my case was active I lost track of Armando. Although it's small, this island has many circuits. You can go years without seeing someone you used to see every week if one of you skips out of your old routine. We have "routes" that we change when we get tired or someone bumps us hard. That's what the city did to me. Thank you, city.

It was almost a year later when I heard from a mutual friend that Armando was living in public housing. I went to see him.

A lovely woman with a fine intelligence in her eyes opened the door.

I asked, "Does Armando live here?"

"Yes he does," she said.

"I'm an old friend of his, my name's Allen. I'd like to see him."

She called-out in a clear, respectful voice, "Army, someone here to see you."

I hardly recognized him at first. He'd lost his fat. I realized it was from attempting to stuff that empty homeless feeling with food. I used to stuff mine, too, with beer.

"Hey, Armando, you're looking good!"

He smiled in pleasure at his new environment and waved me to a chair.

"You like my house, it has two bedrooms and one I have turned into a sculpture studio, don't tell the Housing Office, they would kick me out. I want to stay, has everything I need. You want to see my new sculptures?"

"Not right now, I'm on my way somewhere but I'll be back."

"You know how much rent I pay?"

"No."

"One hundred twenty a month."

"Boy, in Key West? A house like this is worth a thousand."

"I pay them that! A-non-imousilly. Every year I send them one money order for twelve thousand dollars."

"How do you do that?"

"I am rich! But I want to stay here."

He leaned back in a hearty laugh then came closer.

"I have sold the manufacturing rights to El Pulpo! They use it for pumping water out of deep wells in deserts. El Pulpo is bery es-painsif and I get eighty-eight dollar royalty each time they sell one."

"Congratulations!" I said and shook his hand. "You really did it?"

"Jes, I did it. Now I have everything I need. I have found that all I need is love and a place to love. You cannot do it on the streets or in a closet."

"Yeah, the real homeless penalty, you can't love without a place. How're you gonna spend all that money?"

"I would like to see my birthplace in Cuba but the United States Government will not let me go because Castro will not let capitalism take-over the country like here. I have a hundred thousand dollars and nothing to spend it on, heh-heh. I have all I need."

He was glowing. Except for his anger at profit-driven politics, he was a satisfied man.

We laughed and talked about taunting the tourists at the Sunset Celebrations on Mallory Dock. He'd hold up his index finger when they refused his request for a dollar to take his picture. They'd pay Parrot Bill a dollar to pose his flamboyant scarlet macaw on their shoulders for a photo but they wouldn't give Armando a dollar for posing in a fantastic bronze helmet he'd sculpted.

"Take a picture of this bird," was his put-down to the Scrooges.

One twit went all the way back to where his car was parked and brought out a five-hundred-dollar telescopic lens and took Armando's picture from far away when he wasn't looking. He went to all that work just to keep himself from giving a dollar bill to somebody who could use it.

I saw the twit sneaking around and focusing on Armando through the crowd but I knew where Armando would put that dude's long lens if he knew he was trying to steal a picture so I didn't tell him. When you saw Americans as tourists, you lost a lot of respect.

"So, life is good at last," I said.

"I have a house and two scooters," he said, holding up two fingers for emphasis. He used to peddle his wares to sunset in a home-made wagon hitched to the back of an old bicycle.

"Plus I have a beautiful girlfriend, you see her," he added with a macho man-to-man smile.

And then, jovially he added, "You need some money. I can give it. You want five thousand dollar? More, if you want."

A glimpse of the winos and their freely-offered grocery bag of pot passed through my mind. Those who knew life knew how to share.

I couldn't answer for a moment. My Adam's apple stung like a square knot was being cinched-down around it and my eyes felt the same way and I was afraid I would cry without wanting to.

"Ah, no thanks, Armando my good friend. I have a guide business that makes a lot of money from the touristas," I said in the Spanish sense of plucking the feathers from foolish gringos.

He laughed in complete agreement with my characterization of the charade of tourism.

Armando, sculptor, became thoughtful and said in wisdom, veiled in Cubanese, "Stainkaing money."

# FORT JEFFERSON IN THE DRY TORTUGAS: PARADISE OR PRISON?

## *BARBARA BOWERS*

L ike unstrung kites, frigatebirds cupped the wind above Fort Jefferson. Black and white and hovering against a piercing blue background, they reminded me of video game characters framed on a giant-screen monitor. There were no clouds in the sky; no vanishing points with which to measure depth of field. There were only frigates, and I soon learned, there was only one master of the game played in this outdoor arcade.

Without warning, and without so much as a feather twitch, the video-esque game switched on: Dozens of mini-Rodans shifted places in space. One veered left. Another sailed right. New ones joined the free-for-all, while others moved off the screen's edge entirely. Mesmerized, I could only watch, for there was no way to direct the action. No buttons to push. No joy sticks to fiddle with. These seven-foot winged-things soared up and down, moved forward and backward in uncontrolled, surreal motion.

At first, it was soundless motion on a natural blue screen. Then from somewhere, an invisible force began mixing special effects. So engrossed with the frigates above me, I hardly noticed the wisps of hair on my face; the goosebumps on my arms. I hardly noticed that silence had a sound of its own. But with a power surge that sends megavolts through insufficient wiring the wind got my attention. I heard it howling through ancient vaults and gun casemates; shrieking around eight-foot pillars; whistling between decaying bricks and mortar. I heard halyards snapping on iron poles and palm fronds crackling like cellophane. Then, through the din, I zeroed in on barely discernible cries of sooty terns.

Or did I?

By this time, I wasn't sure I trusted my senses or reflexes. Quite simply, the eerie, near-supernatural beauty of this remote island fortress produced a sensual overload.

No longer a casual observer, I crossed the expansive parade grounds, climbed the lighthouse stairs, and climbed right into the video game. Stepping onto the unprotected third tier of one of the fort's bastions, I braced against the 30-knot wind, and like the frigates, I faced into it to balance. The wind roared around me, even as the tropical sunrays riddled their rage to warm me, to plant me as firmly as the prickly pears growing atop this vulnerable skywalk.

The frigates' aerial maneuvers were 50-feet closer now — as if I had reeled them in to me. The ocean and sky blues meshed somewhere out there in unearthly, indescribable shades. And I could swear I heard, somewhere out there, unseen sooty terns debating just when to land on nearby Bush Key to begin nesting.

Amidst the weathered vegetation and the naturally sandblasted magazines and the massive cannons that crown Fort Jefferson, it occurred to me that this 16 million brick fortress may dominate Garden Key, and the National Park Service may maintain our newest national park, and the underwater sanctuary, and the spits of sand that surround it: But the wind owns it.

Backed by sun, salt, sand and sea, the wind's damage to North America's equivalent of the Egyptian pyramids continually keeps a special masonry unit busy rebuilding, renovating and reconstructing the fort. However, destruction is only part-time work: Just across the harbor, the wind and its natural sidekicks are building their own masterpiece in neighboring Bush Key.

This tiny island rookery for frigates, and a seasonal sanctuary for sooty terns, was just developing in 1847 when the U.S. Army Corps of Engineers started its first major, sub-marine construction on Garden Key.

The largest of the five "star" forts built in the 1800's to protect the United States' coastline, Fort Jefferson stands alone in the Gulf of Mexico on 17 acres of sand. It marks the last clump of U.S. islands in the string of keys that undulate 220 miles south from the mainland of Florida. Built on great piers set in coral and sand, its foundation is fourteen feet wide and a half mile long. Most remarkably, the foundation for this 450 cannon fort is built below sea level. Surrounded by miles of turquoise water, and with only three sides of its six-sided moat outlined by slivers of white sandy shores, when you approach Fort Jefferson by seaplane, it looks like a medieval spaceship adrift in liquid space.

Of course, you can sail the 70 or so miles from Key West to Fort Jefferson, as some Old Salts do, and make your floating mobile home a base for an extended stay. But most tourists arrive via seaplanes for half day tours of this aquatic outpost. A hearty few take the Yankee Freedom ferryboat, then pitch tents in the limited camp space outside the fort. Birders, for instance, come for primitive week stays from all over the world, just to ogle sooty terns nesting.

I had flown to the fort several times on mini-visits, and I had even overnighted on an Air Force cutter whose crew maintains flight towers in the Gulf. In spite of their frequency, these short visits only haunted me: While the raw power and beauty of the fort were instantly apparent, grasping the history and the heart of the monument required more time.

Exploring the natural forces at work demanded it.

But, camping on an island with no fresh water — and one that could very possibly be Aeolus' winter hangout — appealed to me about as much as it did to Ponce de Leon in 1513 when he discovered these desert islands. Then-chief park ranger, Carolyn Brown, solved my problem. She invited me to stay with her, in her apartment.

Only a handful of rangers and park personnel occupy space at Fort Jefferson. Their apartments are built inconspicuously into the gun casemates, and a section of the original Officers' Quarters has been renovated to serve as townhouses for the staff. There are no telephones. No televisions. No restaurants, markets or corner delis. There aren't even trash cans - whatever you bring in, you take out.

"This place can be a paradise or a prison," said national park service mason, Steve Siggins, one of the 16 masons responsible for historic restoration and preservation of national park monuments in the Southeast region of the country. Although he spoke for himself, Siggins succinctly summarized the last 150 years of Tortugas history.

Strategically located to protect the entrance to the Gulf of Mexico, and the growing Mississippi Valley commerce which sailed the Gulf to reach the Atlantic, Fort Jefferson is a testament to the rapid evolution of defense systems ... and to the folly of bureaucracy: The largest fort in the Western hemisphere has never fired a shot in battle; its construction has never been completed.

Intended to garrison 1,500 soldiers, most of its inhabitants during the initial 20 years of construction were artisans from the North and slaves from Key West. Then with federal troops occupying the fort throughout the Civil War, the 500 soldiers stationed there spent most of their time building living quarters and maintaining the fort as a prison for captured deserters. It remained a prison for almost 10 years after the fighting stopped.

In 1865, the fort's most famous prisoner arrived. For setting the broken leg of assassin John Wilkes Booth, Dr. Samuel Mudd was convicted of complicity in the assassination of President Lincoln. Sentenced to life imprisonment, the good doctor was pardoned in 1869 for his help in fighting the worst epidemic of yellow fever that ravaged the prison. As I followed the self-guiding tour through row after row after row of arched openings, Dr. Mudd's cool, damp cell swarmed with more ghosts than the other vaulted chambers. Surely the beauty of the tropics hadn't escaped him. And surely, the injustice of his confinement had made his piece of Paradise a crueler prison than most.

Little was done to the fort after 1866, for its armament became obsolete during the Civil War when the new rifled cannon was introduced. Moreover, in 1864 engineers making subsoil experiments discovered that the fort's foundation rested upon sand and loose coral boulders — not upon a solid coral reef as originally thought. The huge structure was settling and its walls began to crack, mixing saltwater with the fresh water cisterns built below sea level originally intended to store one and one half million gallons of rainwater.

Abandoned by the Army in 1874, the American Naval fleet periodically anchored in the Dry Tortugas throughout the rest of the century. And in January 1898, the battleship Maine weighed anchor from the Tortugas Harbor and sailed to its watery grave in Cuba where it kicked off the Spanish American War. Some Army troops were stationed at Fort Jefferson during this war, and the Navy used it as a coaling dock. But by 1908, the frigatebirds and the sooty terns had reclaimed the area. Except for a brief return to duty as a seaplane base in World War I, the Gibraltar of the Gulf was quietly left to the birds and the sea and the wind.

Rescued from oblivion by President Roosevelt, the area was named a national monument in 1935, then a national park in 1992. Although it is memorable, Fort Jefferson's contribution to the American heritage isn't remembered by many: One of the most inaccessible monuments in the National Park system, Fort Jefferson is the one least visited. But that's part of its lure. And the intriguing dual role as paradise or prison is still being played out at the fort — most of its 30,000 annual visitors are commercial fishermen seeking shelter from raging winter wind. Anchoring in the lee of the fort's protected harbor, they are a captive audience until the wind lays down and they can go about their business again.

But some adventurers travel long distances just to make their marks. Back in 1935, the very year the park opened to the public, Harry Klefvie and Jack Almond came all the way from New York City to etch their names into a wall of the North bastion.

More than five decades later, as 50-feet of scaffolding hugged the North bastion like braces, Mason Siggins, sung and swayed to a country western tune above the Yankee's carvings. With the kind of care a dentist takes on rotting teeth, he picked mortar from the decaying bricks; crowned cornices with new ones; and filled gaping cavities.

"The cast iron that was built into the walls to make it shell proof — and state-of-the-art in the early 1800's — is rusting out. As it exfoliates, it pulls bricks away from the outer walls," said Siggins. "We can't keep up with the yearly destruction. It would take 20 men and 2 million dollars just to get everything patched, and the whole southeast region has only 16 masons and a $200,000 budget."

On an eight month tour of duty in paradise, or prison, Siggins says the goal is immediate: Repair unsafe brickwork in areas open to the public — "just pick a spot and go to work."

I pointed to a section of mortar and brick that was obviously new. Clean. White. It stuck out like a sore gum. Siggins' response was equally sore: "Hell no, that's not our work. We always lay brick to the existing; matching the natural deterioration as closely as possible.

"For the most part, this old place, which is still shifting, is pretty level. But where it's not, we have to go with the flow. We lay bricks the way the foundation has settled, or else the new masonry shows up like that mess up there."

With no manpower and no budget — but working 24 hours a day — the wind is far more productive than the masons can ever hope to be. Undoing one of man's most monumental efforts, the wind's effectiveness was revealed in an early morning run around the moat wall: Bulging bricks cascaded four layers thick into the shallow water, sunrays filtered through yards of cracked brick walls; in some places, mortar was worn as thin as the knees on a toddler's pants.

Although the exterior walls have received some attention from Siggins' crew in the past three years (the first professional restoration effort since 1935), the outside wear 'n tear does not threaten visitors like the deteriorating bricks inside. So: A huge section of the exterior Western bastion crumples at the first tier. Clumps of brick and debris rise from the air-clear water above the tide line. And, generally, nature is winning the war at Fort Jefferson.

Yet surprisingly, the structure below the tide-line, unimpeded by the wind's fury, has remained solid. In fact, nature has even bolstered and beautified the moat walls and the fort's foundation with seafans and sea urchins; with barnacles and reef building coral polyps.

Of course, in these parts, coral has long been the building product of choice. Mixed with cement, man used it in Fort Jefferson's construction: Its foundation and walls are shot through-and-through with coral. And for millenniums, coral has been nature's building blocks for Caribbean islands.

It is common knowledge the Florida Keys are "coral" islands, but like the early corps of Army engineers, I thought this chain rose from the skeletons of solid coral reefs which formed about 6,000 years ago. And, like the engineers who built Fort Jefferson, I was wrong. Nowhere is the construction process of a coral island more impressive than Bush Key.

The next morning, I swam the harbor channel to reach its narrow shores. Bush Key's inverted "L" shape protects the Tortugas Harbor in front of Fort Jefferson. Its length is about two times that of Garden Key. And the sandy harbor beach where sooty terns lay eggs is rarely tread upon by man. In fact, from the time the sooty terns land to nest in late February, no one is permitted ashore the island-sanctuary until the terns leave in October.

Meandering from the calm, leeward side of the islet to the windward side, I was staggered — first by the force of the wind, which I knew was still blowing hard, but from which I had been sheltered — then startled by the three-foot high berms over which the wind was whipping and saltwater was spraying. Large chunks and fragments of brain coral, elkhorn and staghorn were amassed underfoot as wind and breaking waves smashed incessantly into this coarse version of sand dunes. Dead and dying sea urchins were strewn helter-skelter. Sun-baked conch shells were imbedded in the newly forming land mass. And each new wave pounded another piece of aquatic litter onto the embankment, which, if it were light enough and tossed high enough, the wind blasted it over the berm to terra firma — a rugged terra firma made from things cracked, broken, shattered. Literally, I was standing on a coral graveyard. I had watched sand wash ashore to subtly build islands; I had seen wind erode islands before. But this was the first coral construction project I had ever seen in progress. The design was as grand as Fort Jefferson. The power behind its construction, far more awesome.

I amused myself with the refuse from what must have been a picnic organized by Beldam Nature for her work force. Sea scallops and sea urchins. Starfish and clams. She had even blown hundreds of man'o wars ashore, looking like blue-tinted Baggies in which to store leftovers. Except that everything was biodegradable, a springbreaker's beach party couldn't have trashed the shores more.

Further back from the shore and away from the wind, where mangroves grew, and where sea lavender blossomed, a black film covered the coral foundation. Dirt, blown from across miles of an open water moat — maybe from Cuba, maybe from Mexico — had settled on bleached marine skeletons; had entombed a century of frigatebirds and sooty terns that had died there. Particles of soil had stacked up like 16 million bricks. And like the prickly pears growing on the fort's skywalk, a succulent ground cover had taken root.

In this paradise or prison, frigatebirds cupped the wind; and thousands of screaming sooty terns landed this very night to nest.

# LIES

*ROSALIND BRACKENBURY*

The lecture's over. I sit for a minute as people begin to move, and try to remember what I've just heard. A thick-set guy with a self-confident sound to his voice stood up there and told us about his successful career as a writer. Not in money terms, nothing as crass as that, but just that very relaxed, almost bored tone of voice that lets you know, I do this all over the country and I'm pretty laid back about doing it here in my home town. I know I don't have to make an effort here, and anyway you didn't pay to get in.

I spend some time wondering whether or not he's gay. He has a very nice dark red shirt on with the sleeves tastefully turned back over hairy wrists. In his talk he didn't tell us any of his failures but was ironical from time to time about the hazards of a writer's life, having to get drunk with people, nearly being knifed by the jealous on account of both sex and literature, solving things by taking rivals of both sorts out to lunch. Just so we knew. It's enough just to BE one, he was saying, as if a jaguar in a cage in the zoo were just yawning over and over, really, it's enough just to BE a jaguar. Can't you see what a beautiful successful jaguar I am? These bars? Oh, nothing really. Just keep on admiring me through them....

Later I hear a story about this man's young lover who worked on a construction site in this town and was told at an impressionable age by the Great Writer that there was no God, so he went ahead and killed himself. But this town is full of stories. Does it matter whether or not they are true? Or is the poetic nature of myth what matters?

So I wasn't really listening to this man after the first few minutes. My attention was, is, on my own thoughts about the business of truth. He could be telling us a pack of lies. Maybe he is. People always say, truth matters. But do they really mean it? It seems to me they are usually just as happy to listen to its opposite. This is, at best, selective truth; like soup, only a few chunks of meat, the rest gravy. But we all

---

sit and listen because this is what we have come for, to sit and listen and be told.

I'm also examining the woman sitting in front of me and trying to see her profile. She's interesting, beautiful in a tired haggard chainsmoking sundried sort of way, she isn't wearing a bra and her shirt is partly undone, which is unusual at a lecture, and I don't think she bought her clothes in America. She has some tightish green pants on and a lot of rings on her fingers. I start to think up a story in which a woman is given all these rings, each one by a different man, and what happens with each one. At sixty, there she is, left with the rings. A row of little weapons winking in the sun. I say that to my friend Joe later when he shows me his knucklesful of rings and he looks a bit shocked. No, he wouldn't use them as weapons.

The man on the platform is using his voice and reputation. That is what reputations are for, for defense and for cheering you up when you are over sixty. He sips from his glass of water as if it were half time in the boxing ring. He continues to talk about himself and Lillian Hellman. The thing about Lillian Hellman, he says, is that most of what she wrote was lies. There will be questions in a minute. Will any of us care whether the answers are true? Any more than if he were an actor in a play?

On my way out I bump into Mina. She touches and then holds my arm. She is so pleased to see me, how wonderful that I am back, how wonderful I am looking. I can stand listening to some of this sort of thing so I stand there and answer back as much as I can. She has been longing to have coffee with me sometime.

What about now? I don't even have fifty cents on me but I let myself go along with her, invited. We dodge out among all the little groups of people who get together weekly after the lecture all through the winter, to catch up with each other and arrange to do lunch. We go side by side down the steep stairs and out into the sunlit morning. Big puddles of rainwater are drying fast in the streets. I follow her into the little Cuban coffee place and we order con leche and there is a small fuss about azucar or no azucar and we get it anyway. We sit in a corner like conspirators. I've had countless cups of coffee this morning anyway, but it feels like time for another 'pause-café' as the French so accurately say, when you want the pause more than the actual café. It marks a point in the day, after one thing and before the next. I roll a cigarette, which is another kind of pause, made longer and more satisfying by having to make it before you smoke it. She talks while I do this. I am still thinking about truth and lies and how you tell the difference. She is so, so happy to see me, because she is having this dreadful time with a man who is utterly obsessed by her and calls her five or six times a day. He is offering her a house on Harbor Key worth 500,000 dollars, but of course she has had all that, she has turned her back on a fifteen-room house with servants, now she can't even find anybody to clean for her, she is living the bohemian life in a trailer. Of course you can get used to anything, but she's having a hard time convincing him that life in luxury is not for her. They can be friends, she says, good friends. But she can't bear the thought of having sex with him, which is what you have to do to get a 500,000 dollar house. Which of course she doesn't want anyway.

Who, she says, who in their right mind would want to have sex with a man who has been married to one woman for twenty-five years? He would know nothing. He would be totally ignorant.

I suggest that perhaps she could teach him.

- I? I waste my time teaching somebody? No, I want a man who knows what he's doing, I can tell you. I'm not wasting my time, not at my age. That was what was so wonderful about the one I met in the summer. Only forty, and so inventive. But he's no good because he's got three young children, and I'm not getting involved in all that again.

She sighs and stirs her coffee.

- Of course, all I really want is someone just for me.

There, it's out. I recognize it with a pang. The old, old dream, the one you have to throw out every morning before you even stir.

-That's what's so wonderful about you and Sam, Hallie. It's so good to see. I mean, he's so attentive, he's always there at your side, he only has eyes for you. You are so lucky.

- I know.

I say this adding to the general fictionalizing of this morning. I think how he would laugh if I told him this. But I haven't quite got to the laughing stage. But somehow the word "attentive" makes me smile. It conjures up an obedient man serving up a little something on a tray. Would Madam like anything more? Yes, I can begin to laugh.

But I keep a straight face for her. The other bits of information she wanted aren't forthcoming. I am not giving her anything here, no way.

She says - He's been to my house, you know. Often. I mean, when I had a house. I once asked him to do some work for me. Sam, I mean. And of course, Leanna - you didn't know Leanna, did you? She and I were great friends. Great, great friends. Such a shame ... It's too bad she isn't here any more, you would love her.

I say nothing, roll another cigarette. This takes time, thank God. These days, quite suddenly, the streets of this town seem to be populated by blonde women who were great, great friends and generally perfect in every way. I meet them, since I've been with Sam. I meet them pushing bikes, tossing back their hair and avoiding my gaze.

But I like hearing stories of insatiable lovers and houses worth 500,000 dollars to be had for the asking. I begin to think of what she's telling me in terms of performance. It is pretty good. Her fine brown eyes fix mine, she talks in a low, could almost be described as thrilling, voice, so that nobody else in the café can hear. Not that they'd be interested, and they're all talking Spanish anyhow.

Indiscretions. Do they or do they not improve a Monday morning? Is this performance more or less interesting than the one that finished half an hour ago, a male ego strutting the stage and pretending to tell the truth even if Lillian Hellman did not?

I'm in the audience again. I don't have to say a thing. All I have to do is be the woman with the perfect man.

We leave the café I say - Next one's on me.

- Next one, she says, we pay for ourselves.

She must have noticed I didn't even offer.

Touché. I unchain my bike, skid off between puddles.

At the store my friend Annie is opening up.

-Mina? she says. Oh, it's all lies. It's okay the first time, but not after you've heard it once. I don't listen any more, can't bear to.

She says it cheerfully, like this is a fact of life.

-Yeah, you have to keep changing the program really, like they do at the movies. No good telling the same old one, even if it is 'Gone With

The Wind'.

Does it only matter, then, if you go round pretending it's the truth?

Don't we all make up our stories, embroider them just a bit to improve the telling, hang them to their best advantage, the one that suits us that day? Don't we prefer the lies? And how do you know when something is the truth - when it hurts you enough, when it actually goes right in?

I don't write the truth. I wander and stumble around it and then sometimes I fall over it like a hidden scythe in the grass and its cut goes right to the bone. But who am I to blame the weavers of illusion, the poets of flowers in the blameless grass?

# LAST NIGHT IN PARADISE

## *THERESA FOLEY*

"Hey you, you wild thing." The man rumbled out the words from the sidewalk, where he sat cross-legged, half-naked, skin stained with dirt, next to a cardboard sign requesting money. His words seemed a pathetic mockery of flirtation. His bare feet were black as soot and perhaps the most repugnant feet Molly O'Brien had ever seen. She glared back at him. She had come to the island looking for a taste of the wild and free, but this revolting street person was hardly what Molly had in mind.

"Yeah, I'm talking to you woman." He smiled now that he had her attention. "Spare some change, love? I'll be honest. It's for marijuana research."

A pothead. No wonder. Key West was loaded with freaks of all varieties. You either loved the place or hated it, no in between. She tried to disregard his strong odor as she rounded the corner onto Duval Street, making the sudden shift from the neighborhood of Victorian mansions to a neon jungle of ice cream cone and beer signs, cheap electronic stores and sidewalk hustlers. Two blocks away from the perfumed elegance of her room at the Banyan Tree Inn, Duval was a world apart. The smell of grilled sausage, pizza and last week's beer filled the air. People jammed the sidewalks, strolling, staring, and a different foreign language could be heard every couple of steps. A lot like New York, where Molly lived, but compared to the city, Key West was heaven.

She crossed Eaton at the light and almost tripped over two people in wheelchairs begging for handouts. Dark, good looking men sat on mopeds, cigarettes dangling from their lips. The guide book said people who hailed from Key West called themselves Conchs. But no one on Duval Street looked the way she imagined a Conch would. Everyone looked either like a foreigner, a hustler or a tourist.

Molly wore denim shorts shredded in a few strategic locations to let the skin peek through, a hot pink tank top with a bright fish hand-painted on it acquired the evening before from an artist at Mallory Pier, and a deep brown tan, courtesy of five days on the beach. She wandered up Duval and stopped at Rick's to get a drink.

She was minding her own business, sitting at the bar, when a young, shaggy-headed stranger pulled up the bar stool next to hers. He had hair halfway down his back, all golden and curly, and whiskers sprouting from his face as if he just didn't give a damn.

They talked for a while about nothing in particular, then he regarded her with soulful longing, and asked, "Would you like to come and see my place?"

She turned him down, but he insisted. "Oh come on, you're on vacation." He had her pegged, a tourist out for a good time. "Live a little." He ran his fingers through the golden curls. She shook her head and saw a look of anger on his face. "Do you know how many people pass through this town in a week? You won't get this chance again."

"Forget it," she said, getting up, a bit flustered. She went out to the street, moving on, looking for another bar, where she wouldn't be hassled by a horny local who thought all tourists were easy marks.

Across the street from Sloppy Joe's, she heard music blaring. She crossed over and weaved her way through a crowd drinking on the asphalt parking lot in front of the Hog's Breath Saloon. Inside, Molly sidled up to the main bar, the one with a tree growing up the center and the broken half of a canoe over it.

"What kind of fish is that?" asked a man sitting at the bar. He jabbed a finger toward her chest. He was grossly overweight with a face mostly hidden under a furry beard from which a pipe protruded. Just another son of a son of a sailor.

"Parrotfish," she said, trying to sound discouraging. He just stared with beady eyes peering out from a hairy face.

The man leaned toward Molly. "Lady, whatsa matter with your eye?"

Molly touched the tender skin beneath her eye socket. "None of your business," she said haughtily. The bruise must be more obvious than she had realized, despite her attempt to cover it with thick make-up. Well, who cared what all these strangers thought anyway. She wasn't going to let a black eye keep her locked up in the room.

She waved at the bartender. When he came over she asked him to make her a drink. "I don't know what I want," she said. "What do people around here like?"

"How about a Screaming Orgasm?" he said, smiling at her.

"I've heard about those. They knock you on your ass. It's much too early," she said. "What else have you got?"

"Okay, then, Sand in Your Crotch," he continued.

"Sounds like it might hurt a little," she said.

"You ever try a Sex on the Beach?" the bartender asked. "You'd like it."

She nodded and waited for him to make it. Spotting a familiar female silhouette across the room, Molly carried the Sex on the Beach over, wondering how Allison had escaped Ralph and John. She nudged the woman from behind, but when she turned, Molly saw that it was a case of mistaken identity. She had Allison's long yellow hair and shapely figure, but she wasn't Allison.

"Sorry, sorry, I thought you were someone else," Molly said to the woman, who continued to stare at her as if she expected something more, sizing Molly up. She had long sunstreaked hair and one of those legendary hourglass figures.

"It's quite alright," said the blonde. "Happens all the time. I'm Skippy. Now you know me."

Molly asked her a few questions, her embarrassment fading, and then Skippy said, "Join me in a shooter?"

"Why not?" Molly answered.

"Two Blow Jobs," Skippy said to the bartender. "My friend will have one too," she added, nodding her sun-bronzed face toward Molly.

"A blow job? Is sex all anyone thinks of around here?" Molly asked.

"Could be, darlin'," Skippy said, raising her glass in a toast. Then Skippy turned her attention toward the stage. A tough looking woman in a see through black shirt played bass guitar, surrounded by a bunch of men with guitars and bushy hair. Molly looked around the bar. It was well stocked with sultry looking women, all sizes and colors, looking hot enough that smoke ought to be pouring out of their heads. In comparison, the men, with their ponytails and baseball caps and sullen stares down into their drinks, looked like a collection of drowned rats.

Molly wasn't into women as a rule, but the ones in this place were easier on the eye than the scuffy lot of men.

An urgent pressure in the region of her bladder sent her in search of the ladies room. Molly waited in line until the one toilet that still had a door on its hinges was free. She balanced herself over a unhygenic looking toilet bowl, the balancing act being rather tricky since she felt a little tipsy from the two drinks. When she came out, she rinsed her hands in cold water. No paper towels, so she dried off on her shorts. She looked in the mirror. Heavy foundation smeared around one eye didn't hide the dark black circle from where John had socked her roughly 48 hours ago. She wouldn't let the bastard ruin her vacation. It was bad enough she was going to have to hide out back home until the shiner faded.

She wasn't even exactly sure how it happened or what they were fighting about. They'd finished eating Thai food at the little outdoor cafe on Green Street, washed down by three or four rounds of Thai beer. Before that, there were margaritas at Jimmy Buffett's bar and frozen drinks at sunset. All the booze was the only excuse John had the next day when he apologized for dragging her up Green Street after dinner, telling her she'd better behave.

Ralph had run interference while John went to town on her head. Ralph kept the bystanders at bay. "Butt out. Domestic disturbance," Ralph barked, while Molly had staggered, trying to get away and yelling, "Leave me alone." The cops finally showed up and took John away in one of the blue and white squad cars. A polite officer with a crew cut handed her a victim's rights pamphlet and that ended the excitement. Molly went back to the room and deadbolted the door, deciding then and there that she didn't need a boyfriend to have a good time.

That's how she ended up alone. Just thinking about him made her thirsty. At the bar, the bartender came right up, treating her like a regular now. "Make you another one, good looking?" he asked, openly flirting.

"I'll try that Screaming Orgasm this time, please," she said, smoothing damp tendrils of hair behind her ears. He made the drink so strong that it seemed to sear her sinuses, so that she had to suck in air to clear the burning from her throat.

By now, John, Ralph and Allison would be at Antonio's or La Trattoria, polishing off lobster, fettuccine and several bottles of fine imported wine. "To the gang," she said, finishing her drink in one big swallow.

The Screaming Orgasm did the trick. Molly felt something snap free, and she assumed it was her attitude, which now floated away in a cloud just like the smoke in the bar. Her usual edgy nervousness was gone as if some psychic sixth sense had told her that tonight, everything would be okay.

Molly took stock of her situation. She was drinking a mixture named after some sexual depravity or ecstacy, depending on how you looked at it, surrounded by people who either were complete strangers or potential soulmates, depending on how you looked at it. It was all in your attitude, and hers was due for a change. Wouldn't it be wild if she moved here? John liked to tell her, "You're too uptight." Moving to paradise without him would show who was uptight.

Molly decided to dance alone, without waiting for an invitation from one of the men who were ogling the available women from the sidelines. She was only alone for a minute before one of the bystanders came out to the dance floor and tried to move with her. It felt like dancing with an octopus, all clammy, his arms like tentacles on her skin. Molly pushed him off and began to circle fast so that he couldn't get hold of her again.

She swayed and moved her arms, all snaky like she'd watched younger girls doing, eyes closed, the rhythm soaking her body like the hot sun had all week. She ran her hands over a bare sunburned midriff. She wasn't too old for this, never would be.

Molly kept her eyes closed, spinning solo around the floor. She might be a little out of control, but what did it matter here? All those eyes were on her, men's eyes, women's eyes as well. She imagined getting a job at the strip club down the street, where they'd have to pay to watch her. She'd grow her hair long. She'd get a tattoo, maybe a chain of dolphins around her ankle. The thought of a nipple ring to maximize her tips sent a pleasant little shiver through her. When the song ended, she waltzed confidently off the floor.

The hour was late. Vacation was almost over. Soon the coconut ice cream clouds and breezes as sweet as the breath of a goddess would be but a memory. The morning flight out seemed to be rushing at her. A night cap would stretch out her little adventure.

Molly went to the bar and asked for a Sand in Your Crotch. Skippy was still there, lighting up the dreary bar like a patch of sunshine in a thunderstorm.

"Here's to new friends," Molly said, raising her glass. "Do you live here?"

Skippy nodded, thick golden hair shimmering in the dim light as her head bobbed. Molly thought she looked like a princess. "How about you?"

"Thinking of moving down."

"Little taste of paradise not enough for you, huh?" Skippy asked.

She wagged her golden tresses from side to side, grinning as if the idea amused her.

"I'm serious. I want to change my life. I want to live like you all do, with endless possibilities. I'm tired of the same old rut. Do you think I could find work here?"

"Sure. There're plenty of jobs, long as you don't mind minimum wage," Skippy said. "What do you do?"

"I'm a computer analyst," Molly answered, a bit hesitantly. "But I'd like to do something creative."

Skippy just shrugged, obviously bored with those prospects.

Surely there was something Molly could do here to earn a living, besides selling T-shirts and serving beer to tourists. She always wanted to try social work and Key West seemed to be in dire need of it. The saddest sight she'd seen all week was a dirty homeless man sitting on a bench in front of a bookstore. He held a styrofoam container of food on his lap and at his side was a clear plastic bag holding four cans of Miller beer. He looked like somebody's grandfather, sweet and harmless, with shaggy graying hair and a small wrinkled face. The man didn't see her, since his eyes were closed tight as he prayed over his meal. His fingers shook, making it impossible to keep his palms close together in a proper prayerlike position. He concentrated on the act, oblivious to his tremors, or how bad he smelled, or Molly's presence.

She leaned against the bar, wondering about the little old man's story. Had he come down here on vacation, like her? How did he end up in such sad condition? Then John came up, looking annoyed instead of delighted to find her. He cupped his hand around her ear. "Where've you been, babe? You're ruining our vacation," he yelled, his breath heavy with garlic and wine. "The others are beginning to notice your strange behavior."

She pulled back and tried to look surprised.

"Ralph wants to know if you're an alcoholic," John said. "You ought to come sit with us. Show the gang that nothing's wrong."

"Why would anything be wrong?" she asked, sarcastically. She tilted her head to maximize his view of her shiner. "Looks great, doesn't it? Find somebody else to use as your punching bag. I'm staying."

"Punching bag? Honey, it was an accident. What do you mean staying?"

"Staying here, in Key West. You can go back without me. I'm staying here in Paradise."

John's face assumed the expression of a lost puppy. "For a few more days?"

"No, forever."

"How much have you had to drink, babe?" John asked. He picked up her empty cup and looked into it as though the bottom held a clue. "You're drunk, babe," he declared.

Molly winced. "Would you quit calling me babe? You go sit with the gang. I'm fine by myself."

For a second, John looked like he was going to argue, then he just shrugged and stomped away. Molly leaned against the bar. Skippy had been watching the confrontation and now she came down.

"That guy bothering you?" Skippy asked.

"Not any more," Molly said.

"Let's get out of here. What do you say?" she said.

"I say, babes gotta stick together." Molly felt like she'd boarded a fast moving train that wasn't about to stop and let her off. She decided to just enjoy the ride. "Let's go."

They went out to Duval and turned toward Sloppy Joe's. The strip was crowded with pedestrians and traffic, but the action seemed to have gone into slow motion. Strangers on the street were giving each other long meaningful stares.

Just past Sloppy Joe's, a young man flagged the two women down. His head had been shaved on the sides and a long blonde swatch hung down like an invitation to be scalped. He gave them an intense stare and chanted, "Three bars, rock bottom prices, naked women, butt naked women." He intoned his mantra until he'd hypnotized them into following his pointing finger down a narrow corridor. Down it, a series of small themed bars was strung together, each one darker and ranker than the one before it.

The first bar throbbed with headbanger music. Skippy stopped in it, pulled a small role of cash out of her pocket and paid for two Heinekens, handing one to Molly. She then led her by the hand up a flight of stairs. On the second floor, a large man sat behind an even larger counter where he collected a cover charge for yet another club. Inside, the air was smoky and neon lights illuminated the customers, who stared transfixed at a woman writhing onstage at the far end of the room. Disco music blared. The man gave her a gap-toothed grin as she read the sign behind him. "Ladies, no cover. Men, $5."

"Go on in, ladies. They won't bite," he said, looking at the two of them like they were a box of bon-bons.

"Let's check it out. I have friends here. They come here all the time. You'll like them, party all night boys with lots of money. Free drinks the rest of the night. Let's see if they're around," Skippy said, nudging Molly through the doorway.

Inside, Molly made her way across the room to an empty bar seat. Skippy disappeared in the direction of the ladies room, leaving Molly to watch the dancers. On stage, a statuesque brunette wearing nothing but a silver belly button ring swivelled around a fireman's pole. Dancers on break mixed with customers around the room.

A well-built woman, perfectly bronzed, no bikini lines in the usual places, brushed past Molly. She wore red pasties and a little G-string with a patriotic stars and stripes pattern, and Molly couldn't stop herself from staring, hard as she tried not to. She didn't want to give away the fact that this was her first time. "Would you like a private dance?" the stripper asked rather nonchalantly, as though she'd asked for the time. Molly shook her head no.

The stripper turned away, brushing past Molly again, her touch like an electrical jolt. The stripper's skin was smooth and brown like one of those perfect pears that grocers display on their own private bed of tissue paper. Much nicer than John's hairy epidermis, all dotty red with a rash that had only turned redder with his week in the sun. Molly thought that if she were a man, the dancer would be irresistible. The idea made her dizzy, and she took a long slug out of the Heineken to settle her nerves.

Skippy came back and another dancer approached, throwing her arms around Skippy's compact waist in a friendly hug. Skippy introduced the woman as Cassandra. "Come by the house later," Skippy said, planting a warm kiss on Cassandra's face, close to her lips, dangerously close.

Skippy put her arm around Molly's neck and guided her out the door to the street. "Let's go. I want to show you my place."

With the words came a sense of deja vu. Molly thought of the blonde adonis's invitation, the first pickup line of the night, way back when in Rick's, but now she felt a genuine desire to see how a Conch lived. The two women wended their way through Old Town, past the Victorian homes trimmed in gingerbread and down the sidewalks shaded by huge spooky trees that trailed vines and moss. Skippy led her to a small lane lined with palms that grew lush and narrowed the passageway to a large house with a wide wooden porch. Skippy scooted aside two sleeping cats, her silky blond hair swinging in the moonlight, and unlocked the front door. "Home sweet home," she said, winking.

Inside, the house was airy and spacious with high ceilings and French doors that spilled out onto a garden and pool. Skippy opened the doors and yanked the metal chains that dangled into the center of each room to get the ceiling fans spinning.

She settled down next to Molly on a big soft couch with a bright tropical floral pattern. The flowers were lime and orange and seemed to vibrate under Molly's unsteady gaze.

"Your couch is making me sick," Molly said, her head spinning. "Can I have some water?"

"Sure," Skippy said, getting up to fetch it. "Do you want to go for swim? Cool off?"

"No, I think I'll just sit for a minute," Molly said, a bit apprehensive. Something wasn't right.

"Give me your feet," Skippy said, bending down to lift Molly's feet onto the sofa. She took Molly's sandals off and rubbed.

Skippy worked her way up to Molly's back and arms, while Molly tried not to get nervous. The strong hands, compact and smooth, unlike a man's big clumsy rough paws, felt natural. She melted into the firm, soothing strokes. Then Skippy's hands moved around her torso to touch her breasts. Skippy leaned close. Molly could feel her breath on her cheek like a little blowtorch. The tunnel of flowers and sofa and suntanned limbs in her vision blurred like they were inside a kaleidoscope. The sensations were bombarding her, and suddenly she didn't feel so great.

"Where's your bathroom," Molly mumbled. "Quick."

Skippy must have known what was coming because she pulled Molly to her feet with one smooth motion, propelling her down a narrow hall to a small, spotless powder room, where Molly sat on the floor with her cheek against a cool white porcelain bowl. Finally, she vomited into the bowl, something that felt dirty, shameful and greatly relieving all at the same time. Molly stayed in the dark room for what seemed an eternity, before she could get to her feet, rinse her face in cool water and walk back to the main room.

"A mistake to come here," Molly mumbled, "Sorry, sorry." She picked up her sandals as she headed toward the door.

She heard Skippy calling to her as she closed the door, "Hey Molly, come back. I thought you wanted to move here. I thought you wanted to change your life. Aren't you even going to give it a chance?"

Skippy had turned on music, and the rock lyrics were screaming: "Should I stay or should I go? If I go there will be trouble. If I stay it will be double."

Molly walked out the door, down the pretty little lane. She was halfway to the corner when she heard the palm fronds overhead rustle noisily in the wind. Up between the branches, she saw clear black velvet sky and a hundred diamond stars twinkling overhead. The night was glorious, with a warm breeze tickling her skin. She needed to think about her options. She sat down on a small brick wall and studied her bare feet, mysteriously stained with mud. She remembered the dirty skin of the beggar, the one she'd ignored at evening's start. The more she considered her two sturdy reliable feet, the more they looked like his.

The first pink hints of daylight were appearing in the sky in the East. Molly got up slowly, creakily, like an old lady. Did she want to turn out like Skippy? If she stayed, would she be stuck selling t-shirts for a living, with the high point of each day at happy hour? She wasn't sure. The alternative was a plane ride home with John, the king of reality. She turned back, walking toward the house, wondering if Skippy'd be up at this hour. Probably. People don't sleep in paradise, do they?

# BIOGRAPHIES

JUDY ADAMS is an unrepentant Scorpio. Her ancestors told stories on their way to milk reindeer and she has been writing about Key West since she came here twenty years ago. She now lives in Lakeland, Florida.

MARGIT BISZTRAY has a B.A. in Art History from St. Olaf College in Minnesota. She has traveled in Asia and Europe and wrote a book about her year as an English teacher in Osaka, Japan. She has lived in Key West three years, long enough to fall in love, give birth to a son, and be convinced this is home. She is the restaurant reviewer for *Solares Hill* newspaper and attends the monthly meeting of the Key West Poetry Guild at Upstart Crow Books.

ROSALIND BRACKENBURY is an English poet and novelist happily transplanted in Key West. Her most recent publication is a poetry collection, *The Beautiful Routes of the West*. She has recently finished a new novel, set in Key West and Cuba.

BARBARA BOWERS is a freelance writer who has been published in national and regional magazines that range in scope from *Islands* and *International Living* to *Florida Gardening* and *Alaska Business Journal*. She is the features editor of a Key West weekly newspaper, and she contributes regularly to *Caribbean Travel & Life*.

KIRBY CONGDON'S bibliography (by Prof. Ray C. Longtin, Dean, Long Island U.) lists some 350 published poems, of which a couple dozen have been anthologized. He is collected in depth by the Kenneth Spencer Research Library at the U. of Kansas. Short stories have been printed in motorcycle and children's magazines, and his letter in *Crank Letters*. (The Smith Press, N.Y.) Congdon's background is New England, Columbia U. and New York City publishing.

J.T. EGGERS is a graduate of N.Y.U.'s Tisch School of the Arts. She lives quietly in a treehouse on Sugarloaf Key, where she writes poetry and fiction.

# Biographies

THERESA FOLEY lives in Key West and Santa Fe, where she writes about outer space, satellites, scuba diving and life. She has completed a soon-to-be-published novel, *Cetacea*, which is set in Key West, and has another in the works.

DANNE HUGHES has edited and published two award winning poetry anthologies: *The Blue Heaven Outback Reader* and *poetry on stage*, the latter a record of her brainchild, The Performance Poetry Series (Red Barn Theatre, 1995). She has performed her work in various cities, likes doing it with jazz, and hopes one day to write a short story.

ALLEN L. MEECE has seawater in his veins. His grandfather was a fisherman in Mystic, Connecticut and Allen can remember playing about the working waterfront there when it was still a fishing village. He served on destroyers during the Vietnam war and is writing a novel about conflict of conscience, called *The Abel Mutiny*.

ROBIN ORLANDI is a poet and environmental journalist. Her work has appeared in *The Blue Heaven Outback Reader* and *poetry on stage*. She is currently working on *Limestone*, a book of collected poems.

DEANNA O'SHAUGHNESSY was born in 1951 and wrote her first book of short stories, titled *The Crow*, at the age of five. She is a traveler, a dancer, a cook, an artist's model, a reader of Runes and a performance poet. She began her affair with Key West in 1993, where she now lives the majority of the year with her life partner, Tim Morgan, and her ten-year-old Golden, Rose.

WILLIAM WILLIAMSON was born Feb. 14, 1961. Conch bred and raised like his family 150 years before him. Grew up on tall tales, real adventures, sordid stories, Hemingway, fishing and drinking. Now living in St. Augustine, working on a novel and a book of short stories set in the keys.